Advance Praise for
Raising Bilingual Children

parent's guide press

"Carey Myles' new book, *Raising Bilingual Children*, provides parents with clear and compelling information about the many advantages of bilingualism for children and their families. This new book not only provides parents with easy-to-understand and well-researched facts, it also provides helpful guidance to parents as they negotiate the often confusing public conversations about language learning. I highly recommend this resource to all parents."

—Francisca Sanchez, President of California Association for Bilingual Education

"Carey Myles' *Raising Bilingual Children* is an essential resource for parents, caregivers and educators working with multi-lingual families. Not only is she a trained expert in the field, but she has the personal experience from her own family to draw on for material. Carey answers the major questions, as well as providing extensive resources for further exploration. I highly recommend this book."

—Deborah Menkart, Executive Director, Teaching for Change, Washington, DC

"*Raising Bilingual Children* is an invaluable resource for parents who are considering whether and how to promote bilingualism in their children. This book is very user-friendly and is truly written for parents ... ımiliar with the theories and research in this area. Carey Myles has clearly looked ... ıalism, but reviews it in an organized form that can be understood by all parents ... nd cultural contexts. She reviews all the topics one should consider in raising a c ... ıeories and research in language development to educational programs that promc ... ˈacy and biculturalism. A helpful feature is that Myles integrates lots of exampl ... dren bilin-gually and the challenges they have faced. Numerous resources are pre ... ...ɔ want further information. A real gem for parents and educators."

—Kathryn Lindholm-Leary, Ph.D., Professor, San Jose State University

"The information on how families can support developing literacy in two languages was interesting and helpful. The book takes a thoughtful approach to helping parents assess their family language environment."

—Mir Hosein Emampoor, Director, Irvington Extended Day Preschool

"This book speaks to the heart of what a parent who values second language wants for his/her child. In addition to answering common questions for a parent, it thoughtfully delves deeply into what it means to be bilingual, what second language education is, what it looks like, and what to expect in terms of academic achievement.

"Sadly, our nation generally does not value speaking a language other than English. As educators, we must, along with parents, nurture the dream for children to not only become bilingual but to become multilingual. This can only be done through education. This book serves to educate parents as it guides them in nurturing a child's bilingual education. In addition, I believe it may serve to create converts of some skeptics. We must remember that parents have strong voices and significantly influence family members, friends, co-workers, and legislation.

"As a long time Dual Language educator, I highly recommend this book to parents and educators. I especially recommend it to be used in study groups where genuine conversations can occur."

—JoAnn Trujillo Hays, Principal, Academia Sandoval de Lenguaje Dual Montessori

"As a teacher, a parent, and an adult reflecting on my own bilingual childhood, I know that giving children a context and a purpose for language is crucial. Myles understands this, and also that parents who examine their values and family life in a holistic way, including the role language plays within them, are most likely to be satisfied with their children's progress in two languages. The examples of bilingual family life incorporated into the book demonstrate that 'bilingual' can mean many things, and that bilingual language development will take many forms. Realistic and reassuring. Highly recommended."

—Todd Stewart-Rinier, Teacher, Irvington Elementary School, Portland, Oregon

"Here it is, finally! A book we all have been waiting for. This is an excellent reference and a 'must have' for every immigrant or bilingual family. The questions we all have regarding our children: How can we give them a sense of personal and social identity to survive in a multi-cultural society, dominated by one culture? It is an uphill battle. As the principal of the Iranian School of San Diego, I have been continuously faced with this question by the parents. As a first generation immigrant, and father of two teenagers, I myself have been struggling with this dilemma. However, I have no doubt that the effort we put to bring these kids to school on Saturdays and keep the language and culture alive pays off. The majority of these children will be more successful with their academic and social goals than their peers.

"To date there hasn't been a single source of information and a guide. This comprehensive and well-organized book, with examples and cases that everyone can relate to, provides the answers. This book is an excellent guide to raising proud, confident and successful citizens."

—Ali Sadr, Principal, Iranian School of San Diego

"This book will make a wonderful reference for both parents and teachers on understanding the joys and challenges of bilingualism and the young child."

—Noreen Ryckman, Second Grade Teacher, Parkside Elementary, Tenino, WA

"There are many people I know who would love to have access to a book such as yours! I commend you for the work you are doing."

—Katherine Beeman, Principal, St. Procopius Elementary Dual Language Program, Chicago, IL

"One of the greatest skills we can give our children in today's world is the ability to communicate clearly. By raising a child bilingually, we not only make them more employable and educated, but we unite them with another heritage and culture. This book is one of the best ones available on a topic that is too often ignored in parenting literature. Share it with your family."

—Tamra Orr, author of *After Homeschool* and *A Parent's Guide to Homeschooling*

"Refreshingly pithy and down-to-earth in its approach to the complex topic of childhood bilingual language acquisition, *Raising Bilingual Children* will be a book parents turn to again and again. An excellent primer for parents who are just beginning the journey, and a comprehensive resource for parents to turn to when their children reach a new stage."

—Kristina Schuberg, Language Arts Teacher and Reading Specialist, Portland, Oregon

"*Raising Bilingual Children* is a well-crafted book for parents, educators, and others who work with multilingual families. Information clearly presented will help parents make confident decisions regarding their children's language development. The profiles of successful schools and tips on the ins-and-outs of the American educational system are especially helpful for parents who grew up outside the United States, but valuable for any parent with a bilingual child at school. The book also includes solid information on literacy in two languages, the effect of bilingualism on the brain, and the politics that surround bilingual education in this country. The appendix of resources will be valuable for anyone who works with multilingual families."

—Eric Hartmann, Teacher, Whitman Elementary School, Portland, Oregon

"Bilingualism, indeed multilingualism, is becoming a major asset in the global economy. People who can shift smoothly and easily between languages have a huge advantage over monolingual people in business, education, government and nonprofit organizations. *Raising Bilingual Children* provides practical, hands-on advice for educating your children to speak and read two or more languages. I wish I had this book when my wife and I were trying to teach Japanese to our daughter."

—Sheridan Tatsuno, Principal, Dreamscape Global, Aptos, CA

"Carey Myles provides an excellent resource for helping parents thoughtfully raise bilingual children."

—Motheread, Inc.

Raising
Bilingual
Children

A Parent's Guide®

Carey Myles

**parent's
guide
press**
Los Angeles, CA
www.pgpress.com

Raising Bilingual Children

A Parent's Guide®

ISBN: 1-931199-33-7

This book, and all titles in the Parent's Guide series, are available for purposes of fund raising and educational sales to charity drives, fund raisers, parent or teacher organizations, schools, government agencies and corporations at a discount for purchases of more than 10 copies. Persons or organizations wishing to inquire should call Mars Publishing at 1-800-549-6646 or write to us at *sales@marspub.com*.

Please contact us at *parentsguides@marspub.com*.

Edwin E. Steussy, CEO and Publisher
Lars H. Peterson, Acquisitions Editor
Michael P. Duggan, Graphic Artist

PO Box 461730 , Los Angeles CA 90046

Table of Contents

Introduction

They have been at a great feast of languages, and stolen the scraps.
—William Shakespeare

About the book

My interest in how people learn languages was sparked over twenty years ago when I visited Costa Rica as a high school exchange student. I had studied Spanish for half an hour a day at school for two years. As you can imagine, when I first settled in with my host family in the capital city of San Jose and attended school, basketball games, and family parties, I was simply bewildered by the stream of words around me.

One morning about a week before my return to the US, my host family greeted me at breakfast in English, "Good morning, Carey!"

They spoke English fluently, and had kept it a secret in order to make sure I struggled wholeheartedly to acquire the Spanish I needed to communicate. The trick worked, and the lesson about the circumstances that facilitate language acquisition stuck with me throughout my subsequent educational and professional sojourns in India and Japan, and also my career as a language teacher.

For the last nine years, children's bilingual language acquisition has been an area of special interest for me. It is a fascinating subject, with a growing base of knowledge drawn from the fields of education, linguistics, psychology, and cognitive science, among others. Thanks to dedicated researchers in these areas, our understanding of how children acquire language is constantly improving. Unfortunately, much of this information has not yet reached some of the people who really need it, parents in bilingual families. In writing this book, I want to share this information with other parents.

Chapter One

When doing my own research of language and literacy practices in bilingual families, many parents I speak with feel that they have not succeeded to the degree they had hoped. Some parents blame themselves for choices which adversely affect their children's bilingual language development. Others are surprised by the force of their children's personalities on how the family uses its two languages or by their own emotional reactions to their children's language development. A frequent lament among families is that once circumstances change so that the children do not need to speak two languages, the children quickly drop the language which seems unnecessary. Parents who would have described their children as 'bilingual' at age five are reluctant to do so by the time their children enter adolescence.

I also see some commonalties in families who are satisfied with their children's progress in both languages. Many make conscious decisions about how to raise their children with two languages, thinking carefully about patterns of family language use, strategies for keeping their children motivated, and setting realistic targets for language proficiency.

Here in the United States, speaking a second language in addition to English is sometimes considered frosting on the cake; nice, but not necessary. At worst, it might be viewed as a hindrance to children's overall learning and development, and to their ability to participate in community life. Families who immigrate to the United States typically no longer speak their family's minority language by the third generation. There are many reasons for this. Newcomers feel pressured to fit in and it can be difficult to find community and school support for your family's second language. Families who speak a minority language as a native language may feel that their language is not respected and children quickly discover the usefulness of being able to speak the majority language, while the value of the family's minority language is less apparent.

Lack of time and opportunity for language learning is another issue. As a large nation of speakers of a global language, Americans have less incentive to learn other languages. Native English speakers in the United States who expend a great deal of time and energy pursuing acquisition of a second language may come across as odd, or even pretentious.

Introduction

Tower of Babel by Pieter Bruegel.
Courtesy of Kunsthistorisches Museum.

Under these circumstances, raising bilingual children is challenging, but it can be done. According to the US Department of Education, in 2000 at least 10 million school-aged children in the United States lived in homes where a language other than English was spoken. In order to communicate with their extended families and pass on their cultural heritage, many parents feel they must raise their children with two languages.

It is true that in many parts of the world children naturally grow up speaking two or more languages. However, children are pragmatic and they will learn what they perceive as necessary, interesting, and fun. Whether or not they become bilingual will depend in large part on whether their learning environment encourages and supports it. Families in primarily monolingual communities like those in many parts of the United States have to work harder to shape their children's learning environment to support positive development in two languages.

Chapter One

I have a personal, as well as professional, interest in family bilingualism and this book grew in part out of my own family's experience. When our daughter was born in 1995, my husband and I assumed that it would be a relatively easy task to bring her up speaking fluent English and Farsi (Persian) because of our professional backgrounds and life experience. I'm a professional language teacher, and my husband grew up speaking standard Farsi, along with two other dialects. As adults, we have both been successful language learners. The process of raising a child with more than one language has been, and continues to be, much more complicated and challenging than we initially imagined.

There are some common mistakes which even we made, some of which seem obvious in retrospect, and I've included them in this book because other parents in bilingual families shared very similar stories. For example, I recommend you do not laugh if your child speaks his or her minority language with a majority language accent. My daughter entered preschool at three and a half years, and although about a third of the class spoke another language at home, the language of the school was English. One day sometime thereafter my husband realized she was speaking Farsi with an accent. We thought it was cute. My husband went around calling her "my American daughter" for several days. Our daughter did not appreciate the attention and she became self-conscious about her Farsi and refused to say so much as "Salaam!" for quite some time.

I also tell parents that a change in parent work schedules can result in a reduction of the regular amount of exposure a child receives to a language without the parents being fully aware of it. That happened to us, with a subsequent precipitous drop in our child's language proficiency.

Introduction

And when I discuss the frustration of trying to find appropriate books, software and games for children whose proficiency in the language is not that of a native speaker of the same age, I'm speaking from experience. There is somewhere out there the Holy Grail of CD-Roms in Farsi. One that magically combines high interest and low language proficiency requirements and actually improves our daughter's vocabulary, and more importantly—she enjoys. Now lost, it came to us from California through a chain of friendly hands. When our daughter's enthusiasm for it waned, we loaned it to someone. Unfortunately, when she began asking for it again, our acquaintance had vanished and we've so far been unable to find another copy.

My husband and I also made the more serious mistake of not discussing our goals early on in terms of what kind of proficiency we thought our daughter might develop in Farsi, given the resources available to us, our motivations for raising her with two languages, and the amount of time she would spend in the language compared to English. When we began to do this on a regular basis, the tension in our household surrounding language issues virtually disappeared.

Even with the recent advances in technology which allow for new approaches to brain development and the increasing body of knowledge on childhood bilingualism that researchers can use as a resource, there is still much we do not know about how bilingual language development occurs. Like any other aspect of family life, the complexity of factors involved is enormous. To what extent of each language do children experience? When, and in what contexts? Does this change over time? What impact do children's personalities have on their own language learning? What about parenting styles? The lack of clear answers can provoke anxiety in parents wanting to do the best possible by their children.

Chapter One

This book is intended as a resource for parents, sharing what I have learned as a researcher, teacher, and parent. I've drawn on information from academic sources on the fields of linguistics, psychology, and education, as well as on the stories that other parents have shared with me. Over the last several years I've met parents who are very generous about sharing their experiences and those of their bilingual families, both here in the United States and overseas. Some of the stories included here are from families who participated in my research. Others I've met through my work as an English as a Second Language teacher for parents with children in public schools.

It can be uncomfortable for parents to discuss their children's language development, especially during times when children are using their two (or more) languages in ways which don't meet parent expectations or hopes. Parents whose children are speaking both languages well are generally more eager to share ideas and strategies that have worked for them. Parents who are trying to raise bilingual children in more difficult situations may feel, because they have not succeeded to the extent they had hoped, their experiences are less valuable to other parents. My belief is that it is highly instructive to learn about the challenges other families have faced, and by comparing experiences from families in a wide variety of circumstances, parents can better equip themselves and their families to succeed in raising bilingual children.

When I've written about real families here, shared advice from a particular parent or quoted a family member, the names of the families, and, in a few cases, identifying details have been changed to protect the privacy of the parents and children involved.

Introduction

How this book is organized

In the first part of the book, you will find background information on bilingualism and child language development presented in an accessible way. There is exciting research currently being undertaken by experts in the fields of linguistics, psychology, and education, among others, and new technology allowing scientists to observe the brain at work. Current developments in academic research have been summarized into what was most important for parents to know, and perspective on how historical views of bilingualism in this country has shaped current thinking on issues like bilingual education has also been included.

Chapters 8 and 9 are designed to help you evaluate your own family's language situation, recognize your reasons for wanting to raise your children with two languages, set achievable goals, and create a plan for realizing them. The sets of questions included here are intended to raise parents' level of awareness about the family's current language environment and practices. In this way, parents can gain a better understanding of what strengths and opportunities they have, and the strategies and tools that will work best for them in promoting their children's bilingual skills.

In the last part of the book, I discuss specific issues such as choosing a school, literacy in two languages, and some of the dilemmas that can arise in bilingual family life. The end of the book contains appendices of resources of various kinds, including organizations, books, websites, newsletters and other periodicals for bilingual families, as well as sources for books, software, games, etc. in a variety of languages.

Chapter One

Each bilingual family is unique. Advice on what language strategies to use, and so on, are most helpful when applied with an understanding of the family's own situation, including when the family's minority language is used, by whom, and in what context. From your own experience, you probably know that people learn differently. Children and their families bring their own talents, interests, needs, and experiences to the process of language learning. What works for one family, or even one child within a family, will not work for all and parents will be most successful if they have made a realistic assessment of the challenges and opportunities involved for their particular family.

Chapter Two

Key Concepts and Definitions of Terms

Language is meaningful because it is the expression of thoughts—
of thoughts which are about something.
—Roderick M. Chisholm

There are three key concepts for successfully raising children bilingually to keep in mind.

Chapter Two

1. Language is the medium, not the message.

It is the rare child who learns a language for the sheer joy of it. For children to successfully acquire a language, they must perceive the language to be valuable in some way. The language should serve a purpose for them. A child is motivated to participate in family dinner conversation, or to cuddle on a parent's lap with a book. Use of the language should be an integral part of the child's life, and conscious steps can be taken to make them need and want the language.

Children are, at their best, open, eager, and ready to learn. Sometimes with regard to language, they are compared to little sponges, and the first time your toddler repeats a blue phrase in public, the comparison will seem especially apt. However, bilingual language acquisition is not an automatic or guaranteed process and children must have a certain level of exposure to a language in order to learn it.

The more time children spend hearing the language, the more opportunities they have to use it, and the more situations in which they *need* it, the more likely it is that they will successfully acquire the language. It can be a challenge for parents who want to raise bilingual children to arrange their children's lives so that they experience enough high quality interaction with speakers of both languages in a sufficient variety of circumstances to successfully acquire both.

The role that necessity plays in bilingual language acquisition tends to be undervalued. There are many parts of the world where it is not unusual to grow up speaking more than one language. In most of these places, however, it is contact between speakers of different languages that facilitates this. In other words, people learn different languages because they have to, in order to communicate.

Necessity is relative when discussing children's language development. When children are very young, parents can make their use of the family's minority language 'necessary' by using that language with them consistently. Children want to participate in what is going on around them. Using two languages with them consistently will motivate them to learn how to manipulate each of their languages appropriately when the situation calls for it. It may become more difficult to maintain children's feeling that the family's minority language is necessary to their daily life as children grow older and begin to move out into the community around them.

Key Concepts and Definitions of Terms

2. Be Consistent.

Consistency is important. Establishing that a particular language is used at a certain time, with a certain person, or in certain situations, promotes a habit of use. This helps to ensure that children actually have sufficient opportunity to hear and use the language. As children get older, too, this habit of use can help them maintain their language skills. It is not uncommon for adolescents to use language choice as a way of expressing their increasing independence. Although it may seem manipulative, from the parents' point of view, the less a teenager thinks about making a choice regarding which language to use, and the more the family minority language becomes habit for them, the better for their continued language development.

Being consistent about not mixing the two languages will help your children to develop the vocabulary and ability to express themselves fully in both languages. Although, mixing languages, or 'code-switching' is a common method of communicating for bilinguals, parents should take care to ensure their children are hearing the family minority language in an unmixed form. If the children seldom hear the language spoken by anyone other than their parent(s), then it is up to the parent(s) to model appropriate language use.

In some communities, code-switching is the norm. Parents can ask themselves about their goals for their children's language development and use in order to decide how insistent they need to be about not mixing the languages, at least in certain settings. If their goals extend beyond enabling their children to function in their bilingual community, for example, to being able to use the minority language for later employment, schooling, or travel, they will want to move their children towards being able to communicate well in each language separately.

Chapter Two

3. Expect Change.

There will be change. Your children's attitudes toward their languages will likely shift over time. Your own attitude may alter as well and the circumstances in which your family lives may change. Expect it and if you can, anticipate it. A move to a different community or school entry often has major impacts on family language use, but relatively minor events such as a change in a parent's work schedule or a child taking up a new, time-consuming hobby or sport can also have an effect.

If your family can be flexible in dealing with change, while maintaining consistent use of the language, your children will be more likely to maintain and further develop their skills in both languages. For example, in a one person—one language situation, when the parent who normally speaks the minority language with the children returns to work and is no longer at home after school, the family needs to recognize the loss of time and interaction in the minority language. In addition to working out the details of daycare and who makes dinner as part of adjusting to a return to work, the family should look for new opportunities to use the family minority language. If both parents speak the language, perhaps it can become the dinner table language. Or the parent who speaks the language could spend extra time alone with the children on the weekend. The point is the commitment to using the language remains.

Key Concepts and Definitions of Terms

Definitions of terms

Some of the terms below may be unfamiliar. Others can be used in more than one way, or are sometimes used differently in general conversation than in a formal discussion of language. I've given the definitions as they've been used throughout this book.

native language: a person's first language, acquired from birth, by being in an environment where the language is spoken. I occasionally refer to native language(s) to indicate that a person may have learned two languages from birth, and may be natively bilingual.

native speaker: a person speaking the language as their first language.

native-like, near native: skill in a language resembling that of a native speaker. Native speakers may not realize that someone with native-like proficiency learned the language as a second or foreign language.

mother tongue: another term used for a native language.

majority language: the most commonly used native language in a country, or area of a country.

community language: used in a similar way to majority language. The difficulty with this term, and the one before it, is that because one country may have significant numbers of speakers of a variety of languages, the majority of people one encounters in some neighborhoods may speak a minority language. In this book, I have used the expression community minority language to refer to this situation.

school language: the language officially chosen by the school for instruction. Most schools use one language primarily, with support for minority language speakers, either through native language instruction or special lessons in the country's majority language. In the United States, there are also language immersion programs to teach a foreign language, and bilingual programs, in which at least some instruction is given using children's minority language.

Chapter Two

minority language: a language spoken by a relatively small number of people in a country or area.

family minority language: a minority language spoken by a particular family. In this book you will often see this phrase to refer to the language used by a family that differs from the community or majority language.

heritage language: a term similar to "minority language," used to refer to languages learned by children growing up in immigrant families or communities. This term also is used to refer to languages native to an area of a country that are not spoken by large numbers of people in the country. Some of these languages may no longer have many native speakers; some may be taught in schools. The desire to recover and/or maintain such heritage languages is often linked to a broader goal of maintaining the unique cultural identity of an ethnic group. Examples of this type of 'heritage' language include Welsh, Irish, Basque, and numerous Native American Indian languages in North and South America.

first language: one's native language, learned from birth. Someone who is bilingual from birth may have two "first" languages.

second language: a language learned after one's first language by being in an environment where the language is commonly spoken. Examples include immigrants learning the language of their new country, and those learning a country's standard or official language after learning a regional language as a first language, or learning a world language as a common means of communication among speakers of different native languages.

foreign language: a language learned after one's native language, generally through formal instruction in an academic setting. Usually refers to a language being taught in a country other than where it is spoken natively.

Key Concepts and Definitions of Terms

✓**bilingualism:** use of two languages on a regular basis. Generally implies a certain level of proficiency in each language.

balanced bilingualism: occurs when a bilingual speaker is equally at home in two languages in most situations.

language dominance: occurs when a bilingual speaker tends to be more comfortable in one of two languages. Language dominance can shift depending on the circumstance.

dominant language: a bilingual person's strongest language. Sometimes also used to refer to the language most commonly spoken in a country or region as the community dominant language.

passive/receptive bilingualism: occurs when a person understands but does not actively use one of his or her two languages.

monolingual: using one language; another term sometimes used is 'unilingual'.

simultaneous bilingualism: describes the process of a child learning two languages from birth.

successive bilingualism: is used when a child begins to acquire his or her second language at a later stage when the first language is already established.

subtractive bilingualism: when a first language is in the process of being replaced by a new language.

additive bilingualism: the acquisition of a new language with little or no loss of the already established language.

language attrition: the loss of a language. Occurs as a consequence of subtractive bilingualism.

bicultural: having two cultures.

Chapter Two

biliteracy: the ability to read and write in two languages.

one parent—one language: a pattern of bilingual family language use in which each parent uses a different language with the child(ren). This is sometimes abbreviated as OPOL.

home language—outside language: a pattern of family language use in which the family uses a minority language at home and the majority language outside. This pattern is also occasionally termed 'the foreign home.'

code-switching: the use of two languages within a single conversation, i.e. switching back and forth between both languages.

Chapter Three

What is Bilingualism?

*Bilingual: (Adjective) Using or able to use two languages,
especially with equal or nearly equal fluency. (Noun)
A person who uses or is able to use two languages,
especially with equal fluency.*
**—The American Heritage Dictionary of the
English Language: Fourth Edition. 2000**

"Are you bilingual?" I ask my students, who are also parents at a public
school serving a population of remarkable linguistic diversity. The school
makes a special effort to support multilingual families, including the evening
program I coordinate, which is designed to provide English language support

Chapter Three

for immigrant parents. The parents in my classes are from China, Vietnam, Russia, Albania, South Korea, Japan, Peru, Honduras and Mexico. Their range of ability in English is broad. There is a Vietnamese mother of eleven children who struggles to understand and be understood in everyday conversations. A young man from Mexico, who speaks English fluently, comes to class after working all day at a recycling facility to improve his academic writing skills in preparation for community college entry.

"Yes," they tell me. They are all bilingual.

"What does it mean to be bilingual?" I ask. "Why do you say you are bilingual?"

"Two languages!" one says. "We have to use two languages everyday."

This is actually one of the more precise definitions of "bilingual" that I've heard.

It is important for language researchers to define what they mean when they identify a subject involved in a study as 'bilingual.' Parents who are planning to raise their children bilingually do not need to be as scientifically precise. However, it is helpful for parents to have a sense of the variety of ways children can be said to be bilingual. For the purpose of evaluating what they may read about bilingualism and from an academic perspective, in order to shape their expectations and goals appropriately, it is important to be very clear and precise.

In this chapter we will explore some of the ways in which bilingualism is defined, both in research on language development and in everyday conversation. Some of the different types of bilingualism described here are defined briefly in the previous chapter for quick reference as you read through the book. However in this chapter we will examine these terms in more detail. I've also provided a few real-life examples of how individual children and families have experienced these different ways of being bilingual.

What is Bilingualism?

Many people, especially those who have very little experience with bilingualism or language learning, assume that a bilingual person can turn on a dime, chattering away with equal ease in either language. It is important to realize that, dictionary definitions aside, most bilinguals, children and adult, are not equally fluent in both languages, and do not use them for exactly the same purposes in their lives. That is, even though we assume when we are discussing a hypothetical bilingual person that this person speaks both languages like a native speaker, this is generally not the case when you meet a real person who is bilingual.

For a bilingual person, languages may be associated with certain people. A child may learn to speak French with Daddy and English with Mom, for example. Languages can go with situations. A child might speak Spanish at home and with friends in the neighborhood, and English at school. Another might hear Vietnamese at church and at grandma's house after school each day, but seldom in any other settings. For bilinguals who are highly proficient in both languages, who are often in bilingual situations, the languages may take on more abstract associations of which the speaker may not always be consciously aware. Therefore, an older child might choose the majority language to ask questions about national politics, but the family minority language to ask what's for dinner. It would not be unusual in the United States for a child in middle school or junior high school to actually be unable to use his family minority language to ask a question about politics or current events, even though he might understand most of a news program on television in the family minority language.

Another issue in deciding whether or not children can be considered bilingual relates to the fact that their language skills are still developing. Even monolingual children do not use their one language with as much proficiency as they will in adulthood. With bilingual children, attempts to judge whether a child is proficient 'enough' in two languages to be deemed truly bilingual are complicated by the fact that their use of both languages is childlike. An

Chapter Three

added wrinkle is that bilingual children's two languages will not necessarily develop at the same pace or in the same ways. The level of proficiency with which a child uses each of his two languages can respond dramatically to changes in circumstance, especially a new immersion environment, such as a move abroad or school entry.

Researchers and educators have developed a number of different models for looking at bilingualism. In addition to looking at when the languages are learned, some of these models address the experience of language loss or the degree of proficiency children develop in each language. Parents should remember that these are just tools to enable language professionals, teachers, researchers and bilingual people and families to discuss, analyze, and compare experiences. Families will not necessarily fit neatly into one category or another, nor will every child's experience. A child might be bilingual from birth, learning two languages at home, later undergo the process of language attrition or loss in his weaker language at school entry, and still later begin to relearn the family's minority language through more formal instruction, at home, at school, or in some other setting, or by going to the minority language's home country.

What is Bilingualism?

Balanced Bilingualism

What is 'balanced bilingualism?' This phrase is often used to describe the language abilities of the rare individual who is essentially indistinguishable from a monolingual native speaker when speaking either of his two languages. A balanced bilingual can most likely read and write with equal facility in both languages, and has the vocabulary and knowledge of communicative and rhetorical style to cope in either language with almost any situation likely to arise. This kind of language ability is also what we dream of achieving when raising bilingual children.

In order to speak two languages at this level of proficiency, one needs lots of life experience in both languages, and there are some bilinguals who are lucky enough to experience both of their languages in a wide variety of situations and contexts, for an equal amount of time. This is really what is needed to develop balanced bilingual skills. A child whose parents each speak a different language to him, who receives formal schooling in both languages, who spends several months a year in the home country of the minority language or who travels back and forth frequently, has the kind of environmental support for both languages that will facilitate the acquisition of balanced bilingual skills.

For most people, though, one language tends to be stronger, primarily because they have had more opportunities to use one language than the other. Again, over time, the relative strengths of a bilingual's two languages can change, depending on the language environment. Even if a child's proficiency in the family's minority language is not at quite the same level as in the community language, that child has the option to continue improving his skills, even through adulthood.

Chapter Three

Language Dominance

Given that most bilinguals are not balanced in their language use and proficiency, some people suspect the difficulty might be due to an inherent problem in having two native languages. Sometimes people think of human language capacity as being limited, as if our brain were a jar or a box with only so much space available for each task or function. Fortunately, our brains do not seem to work that way. Having lots of one language doesn't mean there is only room for a little of another, and speaking one language well does not necessarily mean that a child will speak the other language less well.

In fact, when a child is highly proficient in one language, he can use his competence in language learning and superior knowledge of the properties of language, in general terms, to become a better speaker of his other language.

Pam, who grew up on an island in Fiji spoke a Chinese dialect at home and acquired English at school. She complains she doesn't really have a native language and as the youngest child, she was expected to listen more than talk at home. She left at a relatively early age to attend school in Australia. Since her family's Chinese was not one of the major Chinese languages she wasn't motivated to keep it up and now as an adult she doesn't consider herself a Chinese speaker.

Studies have shown that high achievement in one language can lead to high achievement in the other. Why is it, then, that for most bilinguals one of their languages dominates? The difficulty is not that the brain cannot process two or more languages as a native speaker. It can. Limited brain capacity is not the issue. There are other limits. Sometimes parents are not aware of how small a language bubble their children live in with regard to their family minority language. Parents themselves may be using the language more, for example, at work, to talk on the phone to relatives or friends, or to keep up on current events from the perspective of the home country. As adults, parents also have a history with the language—experiences, associations and memories in which the home language may play an integral role. It can be frustrating for parents when children behave as though the home language is irrelevant to their lives, which can happen as children grow older.

What is Bilingualism?

If you think of all the experiences even a young child might have growing up in your community and what language is used in those situations, you might stop and ask yourself honestly, how much of the family's minority language is my child likely to encounter outside the immediate family? In the United States, for instance, where I live, there are some cities where it is possible to live primarily in an ethnic community where speaking a minority language is the norm, but in most places one must speak English to participate fully in community life.

Anna's English was much stronger than her German when at age five her family left Oregon to spend a year in Austria. German was the language spoken at home, and, prior to the trip, Anna had done a lot of listening. By the time she returned to the United States, her German had become dominant, and in the weeks before first grade begin, she seemed puzzled to find that she could not always remember the words she needed in English to tell her friends about her trip.

The number of speakers of the family's minority language a child encounters will affect acquisition. It is common for children whose only source of the family's minority language is a single person, a working father or paid caregiver, for instance, to develop relatively weak skills in that language. This is simply because the exposure and number of opportunities to use the minority language are few in comparison to their other language. Even if the whole family is speaking the minority language at home, if children talk with their playmates, their doctor, and the cashier at the grocery store in the majority language, there are vocabulary and social conventions they will learn in one language, but not the other.

Another example of a limit affecting language development is reading. A child who grows up speaking the family's minority language at home and the community language outside, may not learn to read well in the home language without extra support. If the language at school is English, the books in the library are English, even product labels and street signs are in English, then children are probably going to prefer to read in English, because it will be easier for them to acquire. Literacy can be a gateway to other kinds of learning. If children don't read their home language, they won't acquire the necessary vocabulary or language skills to discuss certain ideas or adopt modes of thinking in that language.

Chapter Three

It is important for parents to be aware of the language realities of their children's lives and not to blame children for failing to acquire more of the minority language. In some situations, language dominance is probably inevitable. Giving children equal exposure to both languages in every situation may be impossible, but if parents are aware of the existence and limitations of the language bubble, they can make efforts to get their kids outside of it.

Changes in Language Dominance

When children in bilingual families are very young, their dominant language may be the family minority language. This is especially true if the family has chosen a home language—outside language strategy, so that the family minority language is always spoken at home. Once children start school or daycare, and are spending more and more time outside the home, the language of the community and school frequently becomes the one children favor. Parents are often quite surprised at how quickly this can happen.

Trips to the family's minority language homeland for extended periods can result in a switch in language dominance. Families who are successful in raising children with a relatively high proficiency in their minority language often cite this as one of the most important factors contributing to their success.

Sara had moved back and forth between the United States and Japan twice before the age of ten. She had first spoken English and French at home, learning French from her mother. Sara experienced a difficult transition the second time the family arrived in Japan and struggled to catch up at school. Her family decided to transfer her to an international school and settled as a family on a new set of goals for language, French and English at home, English at school, and Japanese as the community language. Although Sara's father was not enthusiastic about the decision and suspected Sara would not make much effort to improve her Japanese, he felt she was old enough to have some input into the family's choices about language use.

What is Bilingualism?

Peter was born in Sweden to a Swedish father and American mother. In Sweden he spoke English with his mother and sometimes his father, and Swedish to everyone else. Because he spent more time with his mother, at age two and a half when his family moved from Sweden to the United States, English was his stronger language. In the United States he initially tried speaking Swedish when meeting people and seemed to be upset and confused when this was unsuccessful. He quickly switched to a strategy of using English with everyone. His father continued to use Swedish and his mother switched to using Swedish some of the time to encourage him to use that language, but he refused.

Families who spend long periods of time in both countries, such as, for example, a year in one country followed by several years in the other, sometimes report their children will begin to speak their weaker language with astonishing ease and fluency within a very short time after a move. Others report a language lag in which children are struggling to 'catch up.' The degree to which this is a problem depends on the child's age and how fluently the child speaks each language, as well as the amount of language and academic support the family and schools provide. A child's personality and emotional reaction to the situation can also play a role.

If children are moving from one country to another, parents are usually aware of the potential for children to fall behind in terms of school performance temporarily due to the language change. Parents should be aware that repeated moves can also be a problem, even if children have been using both of their languages regularly. In different countries the school systems may be quite different. If children find that they are making another switch each time they get comfortable academically, it can affect their attitude toward school in the long term. They may also have gaps in their knowledge that teachers are trying to build upon, or may need to readjust to a different classroom style.

Chapter Three

Parents can make an effort to present the situation to children as a special (and especially rewarding) challenge and ensure their children's teachers are aware of the situation. Sometimes children who are doing well in terms of conversational language still struggle academically. It is helpful for children who are moving back and forth between two countries with relative frequency to have a stable base in each place. It is much easier to return after a two year absence to a neighborhood and school where you and your family are known, than to start over with new friends, a new school, and so on.

Sometimes parents try to change the language they speak with their children as a way of maintaining a language after a move to another community. Abrupt changes are generally not a good idea for young children, as they can result in emotional turmoil for the child. Unfortunately, changes when children are older are also problematic. Even if they are old enough to understand the rationale behind the change, it can still be emotionally upsetting for children when a parent changes the language he or she uses with children, especially if communication becomes more difficult. The habit of speaking a particular language can be hard for both children and parents to break. Some kind of gradual change is probably best, if parents decide to change the language, with the new language being used at certain times or in certain situations, and the amount of time being gradually increased.

Aaron and Zachary had been living with their parents in Japan where the family had spoken English at home, and Japanese outside in the community. Aaron attended regular school in Japanese. Zachary had not started school yet when the family returned to the United States with the initial intention of going back to Japan within a year or two. When the family's plans changed, they continued using Japanese in a limited way as a kind of 'secret family language.' Zachary understood very little of this secret language because he had been so young when the family had left Japan. The use of Japanese devolved into a code used by Aaron and his parents to communicate messages they didn't want Zachary, the youngest, to hear. This ended one day when five-year old Zachary surprised the family by becoming enraged at being linguistically excluded.

What is Bilingualism?

Changes in the language parents and children use together do work for some families, most often when the change is a regular part of family life and takes place in response to changes in the overall language environment. A French-German speaking family living in Austria, but visiting relatives in France several times a year may find that a switch to the language of the country where they are at the moment makes sense.

Occasionally parents feel that one child needs a certain language more than another, because of school choices, for example. They may to try to support the child's acquisition of that language by using it with him or her, at least some of the time. It is, however, not a good idea for parents to use different languages with different children.

Aside from complications in communication that can arise, language can become an emotional issue. Children may feel that one child is being favored, or being given an extra burden. Tutoring or other types of outside support would be preferable, if one child really does need a language and the others don't.

Because of the difficulty that many families experience in providing equal opportunity for interaction in both languages, balanced bilingualism is relatively rare. However, families who find it difficult to make frequent visits to the minority language 'home country' or who don't have access to a language immersion program at school, should not necessarily be discouraged. A foundation of skills in a family minority language, even if those skills are weaker than those in the community dominant language, is valuable. Consider that it could take years of study to acquire the vocabulary, pronunciation, and cultural understanding that children can achieve through home use of a family minority language. As adults, those who have spoken a family minority language at home may find they still need to learn how to use the language appropriately in academic or professional contexts, but they will have a significant advantage over those who have no knowledge of the language at all.

Chapter Three

Simultaneous vs. Successive (Sequential) Bilingualism

3 A distinction often made in discussing childhood bilingual language acquisition concerns whether a child is learning two languages at the same time from birth, or whether the second language is introduced later in childhood, presumably after the first language has been established. There is great interest in the research community on how early bilingualism can influence childhood brain development. Educators are interested in how different ways of becoming bilingual affect children's ability to perform at school and parents also seek to discover the best way for their children to become bilingual.

Many parents are concerned with the timing of the introduction of the child's languages. Parents are likely to hear or read conflicting advice about when to introduce each language. A popular parenting magazine has an article about children and language learning with a headline 'Earlier is Better!' On the other hand, the speech therapist at school suggests that a child's sound substitution problems may be the result of language confusion because of speaking two languages at home. What is optimum for children? There is no simple answer to this question. To add to the confusion, what is meant by 'simultaneous' and 'successive' is not always agreed upon, either.

When we say a child is bilingual from birth, we mean that from infancy the child has experienced significant exposure to both of their two languages. This would be a clear case of simultaneous bilingualism. However, sometimes, due to family moves or a change in the make-up of a household, a second language is introduced later, say, between the ages of six and eighteen months. If a child is not yet speaking when the second language is introduced, is this a case of simultaneous or successive bilingualism?

Research on brain development carried out with Magnetic Resonance Imaging (MRI) has shown differences in the language processing of early childhood bilinguals, children who have begun acquiring two languages before the age of three, and late childhood bilinguals, those who began learning their second language at about age nine. Some experts believe that languages one has begun learning before age three can be considered 'native' languages.

What is Bilingualism?

On the other hand, research on the sound perception of infants shows that by age one, children are selectively attending to sounds in their native language and disregarding others. The results from these two types of research are not necessarily incompatible. It may be relatively easy for the young brain to relearn a new set of sounds for a second 'native' language, if general language development has not progressed beyond a certain point. Children with brain injuries, for instance, sometimes make remarkable recoveries compared to adults, presumably because of the young brain's ability to create new neural connections.

Another issue is that a child can be bilingual from birth, and still be much less proficient in one language than the other. Even though the child is exposed to two languages from birth, there may be significantly more interaction in one language than the other. For children who are more proficient in the family minority language, but still have some abilities in the community language, this early bilingualism gives them a head start on the language they

Arabic/English sign at New Jersey produce market.
Credit: American Folklife Center, Library of Congress.

Chapter Three

will need to cope later with the demands of school. Families who find their children are developing relatively weak abilities in the family minority language should be vigilant for signs of language attrition, as children grow older. Without extra language support, it is common for this kind of 'bilingualism from birth' to fade away in favor of monolingual language use.

What is most important for parents to realize is that, although the terms 'simultaneous' and 'successive' are frequently used as though they describe two distinct processes of childhood bilingual language acquisition, in many cases a continuum would more accurately reflect reality. Also, although most experts agree the younger the age at which a child is exposed to a new language, the higher the level of ultimate attainment in that language is likely to be, it is very important for healthy general language development that the parents speak a language in which they are comfortable.

Parents who do not speak the language of the community where they live may be tempted to speak it with the child anyway, to give their child the advantage of early exposure. A more effective strategy might be to use the family's minority language at home, and to look for opportunities such as playgroups or preschool to give the child a chance to interact in the majority language before entering school at kindergarten. Of course, in families where at least one parent speaks the majority language fluently, either as a native or non-native speaker, parents have the option to use the minority language as a home language or for each parent to use a different language with the child(ren).

Some parents may want to get their child established in one language before introducing a second, while at the same time giving them a start on the majority language before entering school. Again, doing this by having one parent change the language they use with the child can be disturbing for children and can create resentment against the language and/or inhibit communication. Once the child enters school in the majority language, it is unlikely to be necessary for the child's acquisition of that language for one parent to speak the majority language. Therefore, families may try looking for playgroups, neighborhood friends, library story hours, or try introducing the language at home in limited situations, such as with games, songs, or children's television programs such as *Sesame Street*.

Other Categorizations
of Childhood Bilingualism

Sometimes childhood bilingualism is categorized by looking at more than one factor at the same time, such as whether exposure to the two languages is simultaneous or sequential, as well as the level of exposure and the numbers of opportunities the child has to interact in both languages. The table on the following page represents some broad generalizations about how quickly children will acquire both languages under what circumstances, and at what levels of proficiency.

Of course, many children will not fit neatly into one of these boxes. Clearly these types represent broad categories of becoming bilingual, and don't account for all the factors that might impact a child's language development. For one thing, they don't address the issue of whether children who begin learning their second language after the first are likely to develop additive or subtractive bilingualism; that is, whether they are adding a language, or replacing their old language with a new one.

Chapter Three

There are key factors that enable children who learn their second language at school to maintain and continue to grow in their first language.

1) An environment rich in language and literacy.

2) Access to stories, music, books, and other media in their first language

3) Seeing people around them using the language in a variety of ways

4) Opportunities to expand their use of their first language, using it to learn new skills, handle more adult responsibilities, and acquire a more sophisticated vocabulary.

Table 1: Four Types of Bilingualism

Simultaneous Bilingualism: children introduced to both languages from birth, high exposure and significant opportunities to use both languages.	**Rapid Successive Bilingualism:** children begin acquiring second language after the first, high exposure and significant opportunities to use both languages after the second is introduced.
Receptive Bilingualism: children introduced to both languages from birth, significant exposure to both languages and less opportunity to use one language	**Slow Successive Bilingualism:** children begin acquiring the second language after the first and limited opportunity or motivation to use second language.

Information adapted from National Center for Research on Cultural Diversity and Second Language Learning report, Fostering Second Language Development in Young Children: Principles and Practices (1995), by Barry McLaughlin.

What is Bilingualism?

Subtractive vs. Additive Bilingualism

One of the purposes of bilingual education is to help children avoid the development of 'subtractive' bilingualism, a process by which the child's first language is replaced by the second. There are a number of problems that can be associated with subtractive bilingualism. Children who experience this process at school entry tend to be at risk for failure at school, including dropping out, because they are unable to acquire new skills, such as reading, in the

> **Ngoc has eleven children,** and until a recent back injury, worked all day at a vegetable processing plant, attending English as a Second Language classes two nights a week and on Saturdays. She is frustrated that her youngest son speaks very little Vietnamese, despite receiving half an hour a day of Vietnamese language instruction at school. Three of her older children are responsible for looking after him while she works and studies. She says, "I tell them, 'Speak Vietnamese to him.' They say they do, but they're not serious. Just music and sometimes a little Vietnamese television. Everything else—English, English, English!"

language they use at an age-appropriate level. There is also the danger of lowered self-esteem and identity crisis due to language attrition or loss of the first language. For some children, the frustration of having to perform in the school language at a level of proficiency they haven't yet achieved creates a negative association with school learning and an expectation of failure, which results in a continuing lack of motivation.

A truly disastrous situation is one in which a child ends up with deficient skills in both languages, a development sometimes described as semi-lingualism. In this case, the child speaks neither language at proficiency levels appropriate to the child's age. According to some experts, this is actually what happens when a child develops subtractive bilingualism, but is usually a temporary phenomenon on the way to monolingual use of the majority language.

Chapter Three

Some of the debate around bilingual education in the US concerns the degree to which this language loss affects children's ability to function in their new language. (We will look at the controversy over bilingual education in more detail in Chapter 10—Choosing a School.) For a child to experience a lack of fluency in both languages over the long-term is relatively rare, and is usually associated with extreme conditions of poverty and family instability. Nevertheless, it can take three to five years for the average child who experiences subtractive bilingualism to catch up in the new language. There is the potential for children to miss out on some of the learning that should be taking place during this period because of a language handicap. Even children who seem to be doing well in social contexts may be struggling with the higher-level language skills required at school.

Additive bilingualism, on the other hand, in which a child maintains his first language while acquiring a second, is typically a positive experience and is associated with beneficial effects on school performance. Additive bilingualism generally means that a child's first language is already established, and is often used to refer to a situation where children learn a new language at school, while still receiving support for their first language. Promoting additive bilingualism is the goal of most school language immersion programs and of bilingual education programs.

Children who speak their family's minority language as a first language and learn their second language, usually the majority language of the country where they live, when they begin school can develop additive bilingualism, even if they don't receive bilingual education or support at school for their first language. They are most likely to succeed in this if their parents are strongly motivated to help them do so and are able to provide their children with access to the family's minority language from sources outside the family.

What is Bilingualism?

Regular contact with native speakers of their languages outside the family is beneficial for language maintenance, and for children to learn how to use the language appropriately with people in different positions in relationship to themselves. Spending time with speakers who are their own age is especially motivating, particularly when these friends don't speak the children's other language. Many parents in bilingual families mention their children's cousins living in other countries as having a positive influence on their children's attitude toward their minority language. Not only do children have a peer group to interact with when they visit, they're also able to maintain connections with the 'home country' and its language when they are away, through telephone calls, letters, and email.

When children see their languages are valued in the community where they live, they're more likely to be proud of their bilingual language skills and want to maintain them. For children, the degree of value they place on their minority language may reflect the number of speakers they meet, seeing the language being used in public places, discovering there are people studying the language as a foreign language, knowing people who use the language at work and the availability of television or radio in the language. Parents should also be aware their own attitudes toward the language also play a role in the degree of value children feel their language has.

Dr. Evangeline Parsons-Yazzie, Professor at Northern Arizona University, found in a 1995 study that parental belief that a minority language was less valuable than the majority language could hinder children's acquisition of the minority language, despite the presence of other elements in the community supporting acquisition. In her study of parent attitudes toward Navajo, she found that even though there were a number of monolingual Navajo speakers, usually grandparents, available to children and school support for the

Chapter Three

language, children still tended to use English. Parents stated that they felt it was important for children to learn Navajo, in order to understand their culture, their family, and even themselves. However, they were also aware that English was necessary for their children to go to college, and to obtain higher paying jobs. One of the significant, but unconscious, ways in which parents in her study seemed to indicate the relative importance of English to their children was by allowing children to initiate a switch in conversation to English. Parents would begin a conversation in Navajo, but when children responded in English, they in turn would switch to English.

Socioeconomic class can also affect the status of a language in a community, and this is something of which children are quickly aware. A language such as German, which is currently associated with middle-class families in the United States, may be viewed as more prestigious and in a sense more valuable than languages closely associated with more recent immigrant groups, who may be more likely to be of working-class backgrounds. This can persist even when children see that their minority language is used by a large number of people in their community or country.

Sometimes children who are being introduced to their second language at school will need academic support in their new language in order to catch up with the demands of school. English as a Second Language (ESL) and bilingual education programs are designed in part to do this, but such programs may be limited in some communities. Some parents may also choose not to enroll their children in these programs because of concerns their children will not be challenged academically, will be segregated by language group, or will be less motivated to learn the majority language.

Parents who don't speak the community language well may have to make an extra effort to communicate with their children's teachers to determine whether additional support is needed. It is important for parents to communicate their high expectations for their children when approaching with their child's teacher, and also to be prepared to deal with the pressure to de-emphasize the home language that unfortunately sometimes occurs.

What is Bilingualism?

Passive/Receptive Bilingualism

Parents are frequently exasperated to find their children respond when spoken to in the family's minority language, but with their other language. Even when children hear a language often, if circumstances do not require children to actually produce it, they may not become fluent speakers and are very unlikely to achieve native-like proficiency. Some parents who are trying to raise children bilingually complain their children seem to learn just enough of the minority language to get by. In some cases all they need to get by is an understanding of the language. They may not actually have to speak it. The term 'passive' or 'receptive' bilingualism refers to this situation, in which one understands one's second language, but doesn't speak it. (Sometimes it is used when one can read a language only, a development more likely to occur among academics than bilingual children.)

Parents who speak to the children consistently in the minority language, but don't insist the children respond in the same language, may inadvertently encourage the development of passive bilingualism. Children who receive on-going exposure to the family's minority language, but at a significantly lower level than their dominant language may also acquire a passive understanding of the language, but require an extra push of some kind to develop productive abilities, such as speaking.

In the United States, it is very common for adult children of immigrants to say they can understand, but not speak their family's minority language. It's most likely to happen when there isn't a substantial community of speakers of a family's minority language, so children seldom encounter monolingual speakers of the minority language, and when their parents haven't taken steps to create a specific plan to promote bilingual language skills.

Chapter Three

Receptive understanding of a language can be a stage on the way toward greater proficiency in a language or it can be a stage in the process of language attrition, when a child is losing a language. It may also simply be the way children process one of their two languages, with their language development in the weaker language persisting at the receptive level for years. Fortunately, it is possible for children to build on skills they have in their weaker language when they are called upon to do so by necessity, i.e. a long sojourn to a country where their weaker language is widely spoken, entry into a program of formal schooling, or even summer language camp.

As long as children are developing normally in their dominant language, passive bilingualism is unlikely to have negative effects on children's cognitive abilities or to create problems in school performance, assuming their dominant language is the one used at school. Whether children who maintain only receptive abilities in a minority language enjoy any of the cognitive benefits currently being linked by researchers to childhood bilingualism has not yet been determined.

Chapter Four

Bilingual Family Life

Language cannot say everything, fortunately.
—**Mason Cooley**

What is a Bilingual Family?

Bilingual families are not all the same. There are bilingual families in which every member speaks two languages, and some bilingual families in which one or two members only speak one language. Families may be bilingual by choice, or by necessity. Some families are multilingual, speaking more than two languages. In some families, most of the members are bilingual, but they may only have one language in common. Bilingual families include those in which each parent has a different native language, and those in which both parents have the same native language. Bilingual families may also include those whose children are in foreign language immersion programs or who are learning the majority language of the country in which they live at school.

Chapter Four

In some families, language use changes over time. Sometimes this is the result of conscious choices by members of the family. In other cases, incremental decisions on a variety of issues related to family life have an impact on family language use. Some bilingual families eventually function as monolingual families, and may not even be aware of this for some time.

Families who frequently switch between two language environments may also function primarily as monolingual families on a daily basis, but change the language they use depending on the country they're in. In other families, parents may use the family minority language most of the time when relatives visit for extended periods, but family members often use the majority language among themselves otherwise. (These patterns are less likely to be the result of a conscious choice on the part of parents and lack the consistency children need for optimum language development in both languages.)

The following profiles of three very different bilingual families living in the United States reflect the range of experiences families can have with family bilingualism, including issues such as the number of languages spoken in the family, the degree to which families are able to choose bilingualism, and the availability of community support for the language.

Bilingual Family Life

Family Profiles

The Tuckers

Leslie Tucker is a single mother who first began studying Spanish as a foreign language in high school. She later married a man from Columbia and lived in Columbia for a number of years. She returned to the United States before her daughter was born, and was later divorced. She uses Spanish in her social service agency position for which she was hired in part for her bilingual language skills.

Leslie has spoken Spanish to her daughter Isabella from birth. They haven't had contact with Isabella's father for a number of years, and Isabella has never met him. Leslie's parents don't speak Spanish. They live two-hours away and Isabella often visits for the weekend. Isabella, now a fourth grader, attends a public school near the Tuckers' home that features a two-way Spanish-English immersion program.

Leslie says it is becoming more difficult to maintain consistent use of Spanish at home as Isabella grows older. They've always read in both English and Spanish, but now Isabella typically reads on her own in the evenings, she usually reads in English and they also use English with English-speaking relatives and friends.

Leslie notes that her daughter has lately been resisting speaking Spanish with her in public other than at school, and is interested in other school options for middle school. However, Leslie is pleased with the fact that, in Isabella's teacher's assessment, she is currently reading at grade level in both Spanish and English.

"I would like to take her somewhere so she can see that it's a real language, that a lot of people speak Spanish. It's all a little bit artificial for her. Even though she has classmates who only speak Spanish at home, they know they really have to learn English."

Chapter Four

The Lams

Charlie and May Lam live with Charlie's widowed mother and his four younger siblings in the United States. Before Charlie's father's death eight years ago, the family lived together in mainland China. Charlie's mother is Vietnamese. She and Charlie's younger siblings moved to Vietnam to be near her family after Charlie's father died. Charlie went to Hong Kong, got married, and came to the United States, later bringing his mother and siblings from Vietnam.

After being reunited in the United States, the family found their language situation had become very complicated, as the dominant language for different family members had changed. Charlie was surprised to find that he couldn't communicate well with his mother or brothers and sister because he had forgotten much of the little Vietnamese he had learned, and the rest of the family had forgotten much of their Chinese. Although the least complicated solution might have been simply to adopt English as the family language, Charlie felt that would be difficult for his mother and the family as a whole was unwilling to give up the advantages of bilingualism.

Although most of the family speaks both Vietnamese and Cantonese to some degree, Charlie's wife May does not speak Vietnamese at all and Charlie's youngest brother only spoke Vietnamese when he arrived in the United States, having been a baby when the family left China. Charlie's mother understands, but doesn't speak much Cantonese. The Lams decided to continue using Vietnamese as the home language, with family members translating for one another as necessary. Everyone in the family is studying English, but uses it as an 'outside' language, for work, school, or shopping. Charlie tries to speak with his brother and sister next in age in Cantonese, but they're reluctant. His sister Li Wei says, "English is more important now, and I have to talk to my mother. I know a little Chinese, and it's enough."

The youngest boy, who spoke only Vietnamese when he arrived in the US, was enrolled in a public elementary school, which offers instruction in Vietnamese each day to Vietnamese-speaking students to support regular instruction in English. The school also offers daily instruction to all school students in either Spanish or Mandarin (Chinese), and he attends the Mandarin classes.

Bilingual Family Life

The Kofflers

Anders met his wife Jessi in his native Germany, where she was studying. After they married, moved to the United States, and had their first child, they continued to use German as a family. For a number of years it was the family's home language, and they also had a social circle of German families in the large city where they lived and, as Jessi put it, "other mixed couples."

Shortly after their second daughter was born, the Koefflers moved to a smaller city, and both Anders and Jessi felt that limiting their social circle to the German speaking community would be constraining. Jessi described a growing feeling that she and her husband had of wanting to feel settled and connected to the community in which they lived. Jessi was also beginning to find that as the children grew older there were limits to her German and this affected her ability to parent in the way that she wanted to.

One day she was in the yard with her children and the elder daughter pointed to the stamen inside a flower, asking what it was, in German. Jessi realized she didn't know the word in German and, in order to answer her child's question, had to change to English.

The change to using mostly English as the family's language was incremental, though, as Anders and Jessi first tried moving to a one person—one language approach. Communication between Anders and the children suffered, and Anders began to feel like an outsider in his own family. Finally, the Koefflers decided that it was more important the family all speak the same language. At this point the family mainly uses German for certain songs or games, or when reading favorite books, or when relatives come to visit.

Jessi says her older daughter is able to speak German fairly well, and often chooses German books to read, or computer games to play. Of the youngest she says, "I hope she's at least gotten the sounds, so that it will be easier for her if she wants to learn it later. Three of the four of us do speak German, but I'm not sure I would call us a bilingual family anymore."

Chapter Four

Language Use Patterns

Bilingual families often choose to employ a certain pattern of language use within the family. Coming up with a strategy can involve making decisions about what language each parent will speak with the children, or deciding when or where to use each language. Having an agreed upon plan is very helpful, for a number of reasons. Children usually benefit from a certain amount of consistency. They are comfortable knowing what language they are supposed to speak where, when, and with whom. A plan also may allow parents to see more quickly when a child's language development is lagging. If a child persists in using the wrong language for a particular situation, parents immediately become aware of it.

Agreeing on a plan can help parents work out differences in expectations between themselves. If one parent is less supportive of the idea of bilingual parenting, it is good for the other parent to know this from the outset. Sometimes parental differences in expectations center around the level of proficiency in the language children are expected to achieve. One parent may be assuming that 'bilingual' means the children will speak fluently, read and write in both languages, while the other parent expects the children to be comfortable talking to relatives who only speak the family's minority language. Parents may also have different ideas about the amount of energy and resources the family will use in promoting bilingual language development. For one parent, making employment decisions in order to enhance children's bilingualism may seem appropriate; for the other it may not. Private schooling and trips abroad are expensive undertakings and may seem more important to one parent than the other. In some families with more complicated linguistic needs or aspirations, like the Lams (above), parents may need to decide which and how many languages their children should know, as well as the emphasis that should be placed on each one, and perhaps even the functions different languages will serve.

Bilingual Family Life

4 One Person—One Language

One common language use strategy is for each parent to speak a different language to the child. This is often called the One Person—One Language approach, and is sometimes abbreviated as OPOL. Each parent may be using his or her own native language with the children, or one parent may use a language that he or she speaks fluently, but not as a native speaker. Families may choose this approach when they want to give their child exposure to the majority language of the area where they live, and neither parent is a native speaker of that language. Families may also choose this approach in introducing a foreign language to the child. When only one parent speaks the family's minority language, the OPOL approach may be the family's only option.

Whenever possible using the OPOL approach, it's a good idea for the parents to use the family's minority language between themselves. Of course, this is not always possible because the other parent may only speak the majority language. Families should be aware that when the burden of providing a language falls entirely to one person, that parent will have to make a strong, continuing commitment to keeping up the language.

Language professionals often recommend the One Person-One Language approach, but parents should look at other aspects of the language environment their children will experience before making a decision. It is important to consider whether there are other speakers of the family minority language in the area, the availability of contact with relatives or close family friends who speak the minority language, schooling options, the likelihood of trips to the home country, and so on.

Among bilingual families who use the OPOL approach, the amount of exposure children receive to the family's minority language and the number of opportunities they have to use it vary widely. If the parent who speaks the family's minority language is the parent who spends the most time taking care of the children, perhaps as a stay-at-home parent, the children will have greater exposure to the language. If there are lots of friends and relatives nearby who speak the minority language, children will hear it more often. When children's only contact with the language is one parent, that parent

Chapter Four

will have to work very hard at figuring out ways to keep children motivated and to spend enough time using the language for them to be able to speak it.

This is something often not clearly thought out by parents, and so they end up being surprised and disappointed at how little of the family's minority language their children learn. If we take a look at two Italian-American families, using the same language pattern within the immediate family, and even the same languages, the difference in the amount of contact children actually have in each situation becomes obvious.

The Fazzolaris

Paula, who is home with four-year-old Michael, does not speak Italian. Nick, who grew up speaking Italian as a home language in the United States, arrives home from work in time for dinner, when mostly English is spoken, and then spends about an hour playing with Michael before bed. During this time Nick speaks Italian; Michael answers in English with a few Italian words mixed in. Paula and Nick take turns reading each night, and Nick always reads in Italian when it is his turn, but the family's selection of Italian books is relatively limited. On the weekend Nick uses Italian when he is alone with Michael, otherwise the family uses English. Nick's parents don't live nearby, and have only been able to visit once since Michael was born.

The Berkmans

The Berkmans live in a large city where there is a sizable Italian-American community. Tim, the father, doesn't speak Italian, but Gina learned some at home growing up, attended Saturday school classes, and later majored in the language in college. She has a large extended family living close by, most of whom speak some Italian, and there tends to be a lot of switching back and forth between the two languages at large family gatherings. Tim and Gina visited Italy twice in the last ten years, first with their oldest daughter, then with both girls, and are now saving for their next trip. The children have a number of books and magazines in Italian, handed down from older cousins, and often rent videos to watch together as a family. Gina's grandmother has encouraged her to send the girls to Italian classes, but Gina resisted because she herself resented going to Saturday school as a child.

Bilingual Family Life

Home Language—Outside Language

Another approach is the Home Language—Outside Language strategy. The benefit of this approach is that it is likely to increase children's exposure to the family's minority language. Parents may be concerned their children will be unprepared for school in the community language, however. Looking at other aspects of the language environment may help parents in making a decision. If there are other children living nearby, what language do they speak? Are there playgroups available in the majority language? If one parent doesn't speak the family minority language as a native speaker, maybe the baby will often see relatives who speak the majority language.

The Garrisons

"It was a kind of game we made when she was little to make her think I didn't speak any English at all," says Lise of her daughter Celine, now 12 years old. "Many of my friends here speak French, and when one didn't, I would make someone translate for me. Everyone thought I was crazy, but I was determined that she would speak French!"

Lise's husband Bill speaks French, and they have always used it at home. Celine did eventually realize that her mother could speak English, and now occasionally uses English at home. Lise's strategy is to refuse to respond until Celine repeats what she has to say in French.

Lise worried in the past about Celine hearing French with an American accent from Bill, and other American friends, but she has relaxed about this. About her daughter she says, "She knows it is an important language. She knows many people speak French all over the world because I tell her. She knows it is one of the languages of the United Nations."

Chapter Four

The Aguilars

Bernarda and Jose Aguilar, originally from Mexico, have a son who is enrolled in a bilingual English-Spanish language program at school. They speak Spanish at home, and both parents are studying English as a Second Language. Since their son now spends more time at school, Bernarda has enrolled in an intensive English program during the day through the local community college. Until recently they also attended English classes in their community in the evening; however, funding for the program has ended. Jose is a machinist, and uses some English at work, but he jokes that he can only talk about machines. Bernarda has decided that if she wants to work as her son gets older, she had better learn as much English as possible now, so that she can apply for positions requiring bilingual skills. She also believes that if she and her husband speak English, they can help their son in both of his languages.

"He will respect us more," she says. "He will see it is a good thing to speak two languages. And, also, it is better [to speak English] to communicate with the school. Now, the school has some teachers, they speak Spanish, but later? Another school? I don't know."

Bilingual Family Life

Other Patterns

Sometimes parents want to try a pattern such as using the minority language every other day, in order to ensure the children have equal exposure to both languages. Such experiments are not likely to succeed because they are arbitrarily designed and don't allow children to build associations between language and context. It is easier and more comfortable for children to know they are supposed to use this language with Mommy, or that one at Grandma's house. Very young children don't have enough time or calendar sense to keep track of an alternating schedule, and it can be disturbing for them and hinder their language development if they can't predict which language will be required.

According to some researchers, in families in which both parents use both the majority language and the family's minority language with the children, the children often strongly favor the majority language. This may be because the children are being offered a choice as to what language to use, whether or not the parents actually intend to present a choice. Choosing to speak the majority language with everyone is efficient and easier, so it is understandable children in this situation often do exactly that.

> **My husband and his cousin generally use Farsi** to speak with each other, but when it comes to discussing home improvement they usually shift to English. Why? It's because they both entered the home-owning phase of their lives in the United States, and in the US the folks at Home Depot usually don't speak Farsi.

On the other hand, it is common for bilinguals to switch between their two languages when talking with other bilinguals, and this 'code-switching' often serves a communicative purpose. In some families, the natural communication style between the parents may be a mix of both languages. Whether or not parents using both languages with children adversely affects their bilingual language development probably depends on whether the children are frequently in other situations where the family's minority language must be used, i.e. a school setting, or in interactions with monolingual speakers of the minority language. Children who are reluctant speakers of the family minority language may be surprisingly willing to use it with Grandma, or other relatives who don't speak the family's majority language.

Chapter Four

Family Commitment

Parents may not see the degree of their commitment to raising bilingual children and the firmness of rules about language use as being related, but in practice they are. Families use varying degrees of strictness in establishing and enforcing rules about language use. Many families would say they don't have rules at all. For parents raising children in a balanced bilingual language environment, with lots of exposure to both of the family's two languages and many opportunities for children to interact with speakers of both, explicit rules may not be required.

Rules can be helpful in order for the family to establish and maintain habits of language use, though, and are especially important when there is little contact with the family's minority language outside the immediate family. If children have been able to establish appropriate use of both languages early, it will become a matter of habit to use a particular language with a certain person or in a certain place or situation. This can be helpful as children grow older and begin to develop independent ideas about their language use. They are more likely to continue speaking the family minority language as a matter of habit, if it really has become a habit to do so.

Kevin met his wife while teaching English as a Second Language in Taiwan. The couple came to the United States so that Kevin could attend graduate school and they were using the one person—one language strategy with their young son, but were concerned because his speech seemed to be quite delayed. After the boy was diagnosed with some learning delays, the family decided they would return to Taiwan after Kevin's graduation. Although this was due in part to better employment prospects for Kevin as an ESL teacher in Taiwan, their desire to raise their son bilingually was an important factor.

As Kevin put it, "English is a global language, and they learn it at school there. It will be much easier for him to learn English in Taiwan than to learn Chinese here."

Bilingual Family Life

According to a number of researchers, a significant family commitment is required to maintain proficiency in a minority language, even when children receive some support for their minority language at school. Several studies of Spanish-English bilingual families in the United States conducted in the 1990s found that the amount of Spanish use at home correlated with the levels of children's proficiency in Spanish. According to one study, when Spanish was used at least as much as English in the home, children were able to maintain high proficiency levels in Spanish, as well as in English. When English predominated in home interactions, children's proficiency in Spanish dropped dramatically.

Families may find they have to make some changes in their lifestyle to accommodate a continuing commitment to raising bilingual children. This can mean a change in the family's social circle, changes in financial goals in order to travel, or enrolling the children at schools where they receive language support.

Young dancers at pow-wow in Macy, Nebraska, 1983.
Credit: American Folklife Center, Library of Congress.

Chapter Four

Linda Malave of the University of Buffalo in Buffalo, New York, reported that in a study of sixty Spanish, German, and Vietnamese-speaking bilingual families she conducted, one of the most effective strategies parents could use to support their children's bilingual language development was to encourage social interaction with native speakers of the children's languages outside the immediate family, in addition to speaking the language at home.

Parents said they were able to get their children talking with other speakers of their family's minority language through extended family connections, by making phone calls to relatives and visiting the home country for the family's minority language for at least a month at a time. Parents also took their children to cultural events where they were likely to hear the language and meet other speakers, and encouraged native speakers they knew or met to talk to their children in the minority language. Many with young children also participated in pre-school or playgroups in their family's minority language.

Parents in the University of Buffalo study also frequently mentioned asking children to translate as a way of encouraging them to use their family's minority language. However, parents may have mixed feelings about asking children to translate as a specific strategy to encourage language development. Translation is a complex task linguistically and sometimes helps children with development in both of their two languages. On the other hand, parents who speak the majority language well may find that children see the request as a command to perform. This can create resentment toward the language.

Even parents who don't speak the majority language well may be reluctant to ask their children to translate because they feel it puts too much pressure on children and gives them too much responsibility. Parents in my ESL classes sometimes express concern their children's respect for them is diminished when the children are forced to take on adult roles in order to translate for their parents at school, in medical situations, or in dealing with government or utility services.

Bilingual Family Life

Some parents are shocked at how quickly their children begin losing their home language, especially after starting school. It can become difficult to maintain the family minority language when children spend increasing amounts of time with friends, who are monolingual speakers of the majority language, or when other interests begin to compete for the family's time and attention. As children grow older, families are likely to need to renew their commitment to bilingual childrearing.

Chapter Four

Ways to Support Your Child's Bilingual Language Development

1. **Encourage people to speak with the children in your family's minority language.** Bilingual people tend to use the language that best facilitates communication with any given person. Friends and relatives may switch to the majority language without really thinking about it, if they find your children are more comfortable with it than your minority language. You may have to ask them directly to use the minority language, and even remind them after you've asked.

2. **Travel to the home country for your family's minority language, and stay a month or more.** Longer and more frequent visits are best, especially if they result in contact with monolingual speakers of the family's minority language, contacts which can be maintained by phone or mail when the children return home.

3. **Participate in playgroups and social activities with other speakers of the family minority language.** This can involve a range of experiences, including adult or children's recreational sports, celebrations of special holidays, involvement in hobbies or arts, or even gatherings of extended family.

4. **Read and tell stories to children in the family minority language.** It is important for children to see their parents reading the minority language, too. Parents can also encourage children to write notes or make their own books in the minority language.

5. **Watch TV and listen to the radio in the minority language.** Media is a significant part of our lives. Try to expose your children to radio, TV, movies, and the computer in both of their languages.

Chapter Five

Why Raise Bilingual Children?

Every language reflects the prejudices of the society in which it evolved.
— **Casey Miller and Kate Smith**

Parents decide to raise their children with two languages for a number of reasons, among them necessity. Many are anxious their children enjoy the advantages bilingualism can bring. Knowing a language can open many doors. In addition to potential academic or career opportunities, the ability to communicate with other people in their own language can give a child insight into culture and a way of life that might otherwise have been missed.

For some children, bilingualism and biculturalism helps them to understand that behavior can be culturally bound. The experience of moving between languages and cultures may help them to perceive that there can be more than one approach or response to a given situation. It is possible they will be more tolerant, open-minded, and empathetic as a result.

Chapter Five

There is also the benefit that bilingualism brings to the family as a whole. Language can be a powerful factor in the shaping of a child's identity. When children speak the languages of both parents, can communicate with family on both sides, and understand something of the culture with which each parent grew up, family bonds are strengthened. When one or both parents don't speak the community dominant language well, it is especially important that children learn the family's minority language. It is sad, but not so uncommon for children whose parents do not speak the community language to be unable to communicate directly with one or both parents regarding deeply complex issues as they move into adulthood due to language limitations.

As linguist Lily Wong Fillmore, professor of education at the University of California at Berkeley, wrote in 1991, "When parents are unable to talk to their children, they cannot easily convey to them their values, beliefs, understandings, or wisdom about how to cope with their experiences. They cannot teach them about the meaning of work, or about personal responsibility, or what it means to be a moral or ethical person in a world with too many choices and too few guideposts to follow."*

In addition to the practical advantages of knowing more than one language, and a desire to pass on one's family heritage, many parents are interested in the impact bilingualism has on their child's developing brain. As the quality of research in the area of childhood bilingualism has improved, and the body of knowledge researchers can build on grows, it is becoming increasingly clear that bilingualism, in and of itself, does not have a harmful effect on children's cognitive performance. In fact, current research points the other way, to cognitive advantages for bilingual children.

Bilingual language skills have been correlated in recent years with improved cognitive performance in children on a variety of measures, especially with regard to language. According to the Center for Applied Linguistics, a non-profit organization located in Washington, D.C. which directs research and disseminates information to the general public on the topic of language learning and teaching, a variety of studies have demonstrated that bilinguals may

*Wong Fillmore, L. (1991). "When learning a second language means losing the first." Early Childhood Research Quarterly, 6, 323-346.

Why Raise Bilingual Children?

take a more creative approach to problem-solving, may read earlier on average than their monolingual peers, and tend to score higher on standardized tests like the SAT. According to one study, bilinguals do better on standardized tests even in areas not traditionally associated with language learning, such as math.

On the other hand, the idea that bilingual language skills can improve children's cognitive abilities is not universally accepted, as the movement against bilingual education in many parts of the United States reveals. Difficulties that some bilingual children experience with school performance have been cited as evidence that bilingualism often puts children at a disadvantage academically.

Attitudes toward Bilingualism in the United States

Historically, in the United States approaches to the study of the effects of bilingual language development on children's cognitive abilities have been closely tied to wider social and political developments. For instance, early research into the effect of bilingualism on cognitive development was influenced by attitudes toward immigrants and assimilation.

From 1910 to 1920, when some of the earliest studies trying to assess the effect of

Why raise bilingual children?

1. Bilingualism has been linked to a variety of positive cognitive benefits, including early reading, improved problem-solving skills, and higher scores on the SATs, including the math section.

2. Bilingualism can enable children to experience more than one cultural perspective on the world.

3. Bilingualism can enhance children's later opportunities in higher education.

4. Bilingualism can improve children's later prospects for employment.

5. Bilingualism can strengthen family ties.

bilingualism on cognitive performance took place in the United States, many states were passing anti-German language laws. In Minnesota, immigrant schoolchildren were given "Let's Speak English" buttons, in hopes of hastening their assimilation into American life. Desires to maintain one's family minority language were viewed with suspicion, as being 'un-American.'

Chapter Five

In addition to the hostility toward bilingualism, a lack of an appropriate working definition of 'bilingualism' posed a significant problem for the quality of early research in the United States. In these early studies, the criteria for deciding who was bilingual and therefore an appropriate subject for study inclusion was questionable. Some of people who were included may have been monolingual speakers of English, chosen on the basis of an ethnic surname. Others may have been immigrants who had not yet learned English, but were, in fact, monolingual speakers of their minority language.

At the time of these early studies, IQ tests were becoming a popular way to measure people's cognitive abilities, and so research on the effect of bilingualism on cognitive performance involved analysis of the results of standardized IQ tests. It is unclear whether subjects were sufficiently proficient in the language they were required to use in taking the tests. Some studies involved translated tests; on the other hand, the style of the tests and their subject matter may have been as foreign as English to some of the test takers. The literacy skills of the test-takers was another issue. In tests given to WWI draftees, immigrants and illiterates were grouped together, and some tests were administered through signing and gestures in order to surmount language and literacy obstacles.

A myth that has persisted in part from the dissemination of the results of early research on childhood bilingualism is the notion that bilingual children are likely to be at a cognitive disadvantage. Some people still hold the belief that children forced to cope with two languages experience an intellectual burden that will negatively affect their learning and growth in other areas. As a parent trying to raise your child with two languages you may encounter well-meaning people who express concern that your child might be confused or have trouble at school because of his bilingual up-bringing. The fact that bilingual children often begin to speak later than their monolingual peers and may mix the two languages for a time helps to bolster this myth. Fortunately, current research does not support it.

Yet another flaw with these studies was the fact that they were not designed to control for socioeconomic variables, such as family income or the extent of parents' experience with formal

Why Raise Bilingual Children?

education. Study findings were interpreted as demonstrations that 'bilingual' children suffered cognitive handicaps compared to monolingual children. It is likely that the poor performance of many children could be linked instead to the challenges their families faced, such as poverty and a limited experience with formal education, factors which are now known to have a negative impact on children's scores on standardized tests. In any case, given the context surrounding this early research on bilingualism, it is not surprising that bilingualism was found to have a negative effect on cognitive performance.

Statue of San Rocco decorated with money by parade onlookers.
Credit: American Folklife Center, Library of Congress.

8 Research conducted in the 1960s and '70s was motivated, at least in part, by the desire to demonstrate cognitive benefits of bilingualism. As might be expected, studies that took place in an intellectual environment more supportive of 'multiculturalism,' found that bilingual children enjoyed some cognitive or intellectual advantages over monolingual counterparts.

It could be argued the designs of these studies were flawed, too, but with a bias toward bilingualism. The selection of the children to be included may have skewed the results toward a more favorable outcome for children who were bilingual. The socioeconomic background of these children was relatively high, and the languages the children were learning were considered prestigious languages spoken by substantial numbers of speakers around the world. The children selected were therefore likely to do well on standardized tests, in any case.

Chapter Five

Current research problems

Accounting for the effects of socioeconomic class has continued to be a problem for researchers interested in childhood bilingual language development. Research on bilingual children's language development currently tends to be conducted with middle-class children who are as much like similar groups of monolingual children as possible.

In this way, researchers are able to eliminate factors such as the stress of immigration, the impact of poverty, and the effect of lower parental literacy levels that might have an effect on children's performance. Unfortunately, this also means that researchers are not able to generalize their findings. The results arrived at in their research may or may not reflect accurately how bilingualism affects the cognitive development of all children.

Another problem is that even groups of bilingual children who are seemingly comparable in terms of family income or parent level of education may have other advantages over monolingual groups. For instance, some studies are conducted by collecting data from school immersion programs. One might expect that families who selected special school programs for their children would be highly motivated to help them succeed academically, and this could be reflected in children's test scores. Parents might also decide to send a child who seems quite bright and verbal to a school with a language program in order to maximize those skills.

Bilingual children may also have traveled more than their monolingual counterparts, and may have more knowledge of other cultures. They may have attended more arts or culturally related events as a result of parental efforts to increase their exposure to the family's minority language. Bilingual children who attend regular school in their community's dominant language may also receive additional schooling in their family's minority language, for example, by attending 'Saturday school.' All of these experiences could have a beneficial impact on their cognitive development.

Why Raise Bilingual Children?

Cognitive Advantages and
the Threshold Hypothesis

It is clear that children must be able to function at native speaker levels appropriate for their age in at least one of their two languages to avoid cognitive difficulties and poor school performance. It has also been proposed that children must reach a certain level of proficiency in both languages in order to gain the cognitive benefits associated with bilingualism. This theory is known as the Threshold Hypothesis.

The Threshold Hypothesis, developed by Dr. Jim Cummins, a well-known researcher in the area of childhood bilingualism and school performance, states that in order for children to enjoy the cognitive benefits of bilingualism, children's proficiency levels must be at an age-appropriate level in both languages.

Other researchers, however, have found that bilingual children with significantly weaker skills in one language than the other also have performed better than monolingual children on various test measures. (Most linguists agree that, as long as a child is able to use at least one of their two languages at an age-appropriate level, having less proficiency in the other language does not negatively affect cognitive performance.) The point where children are most engaged in learning a new language may be the time when the effects on the brain are strongest.

Chapter Five

What <u>are</u> the cognitive advantages of bilingualism?

Bilingualism has been linked to better performance in a number of skills, with bilingual children demonstrating better listening perception and more flexible approaches to problem solving. At this point, though, evidence is strongest for bilingualism being tied to language skills. Recent studies of bilingual children indicate they tend to have a better understanding of how language works. This research includes studies of children in French immersion school programs in Canada and children from Spanish-speaking homes enrolled in bilingual education programs in the United States.

Bilingual children seem to recognize earlier than monolingual children do that language is symbolic. Having learned relatively early that a dog can be 'dog' or 'perro', for instance, the arbitrary nature of language is more obvious to them. Bilingual children also had to learn to use two different systems of grammar. For many children, this makes them more aware of how each grammar system works, and so they are more skilled at interpreting and manipulating grammar to communicate clearly. Bilingual children often demonstrate a greater sensitivity to subtle differences in meaning than monolingual children of the same age, perhaps as a result of their more sophisticated ability to analyze the nuances of word choice and grammar.

Why Raise Bilingual Children?

Childhood Bilingualism and Early Reading

According to Dr. Ellen Bialystok, a professor of psychology at York University in Toronto and noted researcher of bilingual children's language acquisition, bilingual children recognize earlier than monolingual children do that written language carries meaning, and therefore are often ahead of monolingual peers in learning to read.

In her study of French-English and Chinese-English bilingual four- and five-year-olds, Dr. Bialystok showed the children a word and picture together, and then changed the picture. The bilingual children were twice as likely as the monolingual children to correctly identify the written word after the picture had changed. In a second test, in which children were asked to analyze word length, the Chinese-English speaking children did better than either the monolingual children or the French-English speaking children, an outcome Dr. Bialystok attributes to their experience in dealing with two different writing systems. (The French-English speaking children did not do any better than the monolingual children on this second test.)

Does Language Shape How We Think?

If you ask the man on the street whether the language we speak affects the way we perceive and think about the world, he is likely to agree. This is why we have continuing debates about the effects of the continuing use of sexist language, rather than more gender-neutral expressions, i.e. "the person on the street." Perhaps this idea that language influences how we think underlies the common concern people have that children raised with two languages will become confused. It may also explain the interest of researchers in attempting to correlate bilingualism and a more flexible approach to problem solving. Within the field of linguistics, however, this idea is a controversial one.

Anthropologist Edward Sapir and Benjamin Whorf, an engineer and amateur linguist who studied with Sapir at Yale, in the 1920s and '30s published writings on the connection between language and culture that explored the possibility the language we think in somehow affects how we think. They proposed a theory that has become known as the Sapir-Whorf Hypothesis.

Chapter Five

The Sapir-Whorf hypothesis consists of two main ideas. The first is linguistic determinism, the notion that our language determines our perceptions of the world around us. The second, linguistic relativity, presumes that people who use different languages will perceive the world in entirely different ways due to linguistic determinism.

There are two versions of the concept of linguistic determinism, 'weak' and 'strong.' Strong determinism holds that language is equivalent to thought and there is no difference between our thoughts and the language we speak. Weak determinism, on the other hand, is the idea that the language we speak merely influences the way we think. Weak determinism also allows for the possibility that our experiences shape the language we use. It's more of a two-way process.

The notion of linguistic relativism is an extremely uncomfortable one for many people, especially those interested in other languages and cultures, in that it implies that different groups of people may not, in fact, ever truly understand one another. On the other hand, weak determinism, the idea that the words we choose may influence how we think, and that the way we think affects the words we choose is becoming a more accepted idea. Unfortunately, it is difficult to test in a scientifically valid way.

Whether or not language has an actual effect on cognitive processes, most parents who are interested in raising bilingual children do believe that speaking two languages will affect how their children experience and think about the world, simply because of the additional access to different perspectives on the world.

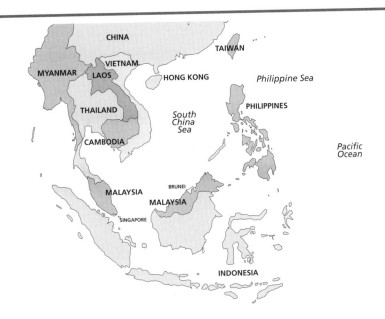

Chapter Six

Children's Language Acquisition: Theories and Research

To handle a language skillfully is to practice a kind of evocative sorcery.
—**Charles Baudelaire**

In this chapter we will take a look at some of the theories that have shaped current thinking about language acquisition in general and bilingual language acquisition in particular. In the past, it was assumed that children learned language by imitating the speech of those around them and by getting feedback from parents and other older speakers that reinforced correct speech. Although this kind of information from other speakers probably plays a large part in children's language acquisition, it is no longer thought of as a complete explanation. It was challenged in the 1950s and '60s by linguists who believed, for a number of reasons, that human beings are born with the innate

Chapter Six

ability to develop language skills. Linguist Noam Chomsky, for example, proposed that human brains at birth already have structures designed to guide the development of language. Current theoretical models of language acquisition tend to incorporate some aspects of behaviorism in addition to later ideas regarding an innate ability in humans for language. Humans may be hard-wired for language, but when and how language actually develops depends to some degree on the language environment.

Behaviorism

The behaviorist model of language learning emerged from psychological theories of human behavior that arose in the early twentieth century. Ivan Pavlov's series of experiments on dogs' conditioned reactions to repeated stimulus is one of the better-known examples of behaviorism at work. Essentially, behaviorism is the idea that our actions are shaped by a kind of feedback loop that occurs between an act and the reaction or response to that act. If by doing something, one gets a positive response, one is inclined to do it again. For a baby, positive responses to attempts to communicate could include attention, continued interaction with parents, or receiving something the baby desires, i.e. a bottle or a certain toy. The idea is through observation of how others talk, and by getting feedback in response to his own efforts at communication, the child is able to refine and modify his behavior appropriately.

Psychologist B. F. Skinner wrote several books about the possibility of using behaviorism to promote positive social change in the mid twentieth century. Behaviorism became popular as a way of thinking about human development, and in the 1950s most theories about how humans learned language were based on behaviorism. However, some linguists felt that when one looked at what was happening with the language development of actual children, behaviorism didn't account for the entire process of language acquisition.

For one thing, all children tend to go through the process of acquiring language in more or less the same way. That is, they pass through certain phases and stages of language use in a similar order and at roughly the same age. This appears to be true even across languages. If how children learn language is predominantly the result of their environment, one would expect more variation.

Children's Language Acquisition

Another issue is that children do not receive as much correction and feedback as may have been earlier supposed. Parents are more interested in communicating with their children rather than correcting them, and those corrections that do occur are likely to be of a factual rather than a grammatical nature. When a toddler points to the fleeing family cat and says, "Doggie go!" parents are more likely to respond with, "That's the kitty," as opposed to "No, it goes."

Also, the speech children listen to is not as grammatical as we would like to think. We tend to speak in fragments, yet children eventually work out from this what constitutes a complete sentence in their language.

If we look at the kinds of grammatical mistakes children make, we see that frequently children are using the grammar rules they have learned, but in cases where they may not be appropriate or necessary. For instance, in English a child might know the word "mouse" means one mouse, and even that the plural form is "mice," but still persist in adding the plural marker "s", saying "mices" to mean more than one mouse. The child has learned the rule that adding an "s" can make nouns plural, but knowing when to apply it correctly takes much longer.

Since adults don't go around saying things like "mices," children don't come up with constructions like this through imitation. It seems that children play a more active role than previously thought in working out the rules for their language(s). Children are engaging in the same kind of hypothesizing and testing with language they use in other forms of learning.

It also appears that children may not be able to grasp certain grammatical structures until they are cognitively ready to do so, a phenomenon that parallels children's cognitive development in other areas, such as number sense or logical reasoning. There are a number of examples in research literature of children being apparently unable to repeat certain grammatical structures despite being given direct correction and prompting, or indirect modeling of the correct form. One classic and frequently cited example comes from the work of linguist David McNeill, who reported the following exchange between mother and child.

Chapter Six

CHILD: Nobody don't likes me.
MOTHER: No, say 'Nobody likes me.'
CHILD: Nobody don't likes me.
(Eight repetitions of this dialogue.)
MOTHER: No. Now listen carefully: say 'Nobody likes me.'
CHILD: Oh! Nobody don't likes me.'

Another aspect of children's language acquisition that is not yet completely understood is the role of "caregiver speech." It has been shown across languages and cultures that parents and other caregivers tend to modify their language in speaking with infants and toddlers. Adults tend to speak more slowly and at a higher pitch when they are talking to small children. Certain sounds may be over-emphasized, sentences are short and simple, and interaction is encouraged. For instance, we might ask, " More juice? Does baby want more juice?" repeating the essential information. Repeating a child's words and expanding on what the child has said is another common feature in this special way of talking to children. "Caregiver speech" is not used in all languages or cultures, however, and concrete evidence on exactly how it affects children's language development is limited.

Children's Language Acquisition

Hard-Wired for Language: "Innateness" Theories

One way linguists who argue for an "innateness" theory of language acquisition explain how the process might work is with a model of language learning that includes a Language Acquisition Device (LAD). This device is located in the brain and provides certain universal principles of language. It gives children a starting point and some guidance along the way in the process of acquiring language. Outside input (i.e. speech from others) is necessary to "activate" the device.

While the term Language Acquisition Device conjures up an image of an intact unit, a little black box, operating on its own within the brain, brain research has shown that language involves many physical areas of the brain. In multilingual people, the areas of the brain involved in processing language vary depending on when a language was learned. For example, someone who grew up speaking Italian and German as a child, and learned English as an adult, would use different parts of the brain for the processing of English than his or her 'native' languages of German and Italian. The Language Acquisition Device, if it exists, is probably more accurately thought of as being made up of a number of different physical parts of the brain working as a system, all involved in language processing and development.

Chapter Six

The Critical Period Hypothesis

Most linguists now agree that both nature and nurture play significant roles in human language development, although how much of each factor and how this interaction occurs are still subject to debate. A new area of theoretical inquiry has centered on the growing evidence there are deadlines for many aspects of cognitive development. Many programs aimed at promoting school readiness are based on research indicating that early cognitive development affects children's later learning. For parents in bilingual families, the ongoing discussion about the possibility of a critical period is important because of the implications for their children's language development, and even their ability to learn new languages later in life.

Psycholinguist Eric Lenneberg is one of the better-known early proponents of a theory concerning how language development occurs in children, which is generally known as the critical period hypothesis. Lenneberg believed that language was innate, but required certain stimulus in order to begin development. In other words, the brains of human infants are ready to learn language, but language development doesn't occur unless caregivers talk to and interact with the child. The important element introduced in the critical period hypothesis is that if a child is not exposed to language *by a certain age*, language will not develop normally. This would imply that when people try to learn languages after a certain age, they are struggling against a real handicap related perhaps to stages in cognitive development.

According to some estimates, about five percent of adult language learners are able to achieve native or near native-like proficiency in a second language. It is not yet known why these adults are able to achieve more success than the average adult language learner, but factors are likely to include the situation in which they acquire the second language, degree of motivation, and individual talents and abilities. Just as some of us are more talented in music, math, or athletics, some have a particular gift for languages.

Children's Language Acquisition

Are children better language learners? Parents in families who have moved to a new country often feel that their children are learning their new language with enviable speed and ease. It is common for children to pick up a new language more quickly than their parents, and, in the end, to speak it better. This in and of itself doesn't prove that their advantage is due to having a younger brain.

The factors resulting in differences in acquisition and proficiency levels for different individuals are complex and not limited to age difference alone. For instance, adults have work and family responsibilities which may limit their language learning opportunities, while children are often at school, essentially an immersion environment. Children may also experience stronger motivation to learn because of their desire to interact with other children. They may also be less conflicted than their parents about feelings toward the new language. Language can be a strong component of our identity. Children, who are in the process of creating their adult identities, may be more easily able to view themselves as speakers, or owners, of the new language.

There is growing acceptance of the idea there is a window of opportunity or a 'critical period' during which a person's brain is unusually receptive to language learning. The theory is the brain's structure develops to process the language a person knows and as time passes becomes increasingly less able to accommodate a new language. At issue may be the degree to which the brain can create new neural connections to process a new language or the extent to which connections set up to process one language can be used for the processing of a new one. Although we know that people's brains can create new synaptic connections while learning at any age, the process slows. One way to think of the critical period is simply to imagine a gradual decline in one's ability to acquire new languages.

Chapter Six

Another idea is that it is actually a set of critical periods, with different "deadlines" for various aspects of language development, such as syntax (grammar), pronunciation, and vocabulary. Researchers have used a number of approaches to try to determine exactly when these deadlines for language development occur, including examination of case studies of children who were deprived of normal language stimulation, study of the recoveries of brain injury patients, and Magnetic Resonance Imaging (MRI) scans of healthy brains at work.

Some of this research points to the onset of puberty as a possible "cut-off" date for development of a normal language processing system. Other research, on second language learners, shows a more gradual decline in eventual achievement in the new language, depending on how old the learner is when the new language is first introduced. The younger a child is when first exposed to a language, the higher his or her proficiency in the language is likely to be.

Beyond childhood, relative age doesn't seem to affect how well one learns a language, but adults are not likely to reach the level of proficiency that children do. In other words, for adults it doesn't seem to matter so much whether one is forty or fifty when learning a new language, but a child who starts a new language at one year of age has a significant advantage over a ten-year-old. And the ten-year-old is likely to eventually speak the language better than either the forty- or fifty-year-old.

Children's Language Acquisition

The Developing Brain

It may be that our capacity for learning a new language begins to decrease as soon as we start to learn our native language(s). An important factor at work is the brain's relative plasticity when we are young. An infant starts out with an abundance of synaptic connections with the potential for involvement in language processing. As the infant begins to specialize in his native language(s), the synaptic connections that are needed become stronger, while those that are not used die off and the brain's ability to create new systems diminishes, as fewer synapses are available.

In studies of brain injury patients, those who were injured as children were better able to recover language functioning, as well as other types of cognitive functioning, than those who were injured as adults. It is likely that this is due to younger brains' ability to create new synaptic systems to take over from damaged systems.

It is known that for some aspects of cognitive functioning, at least in animals, the brain must develop those functions by a particular stage of physical development. The phrase "use it or lose it," has been applied to brain functioning in adulthood; in young brains, it may be that one has a deadline. If the brain hasn't received certain triggers or experiences in time, normal functioning will not develop.

Experiments with kittens demonstrated if they didn't receive normal stimulation of the visual cortex within a certain critical period, they don't develop normal visual functioning, even though the eye itself is undamaged. Although vision in these cats may improve somewhat over time, the cats never develop normal vision. Similar experiments have been done with other animals, with comparable results.

Chapter Six

According to Dr. Susan Curtiss, a linguist at the University of California at Los Angeles (UCLA), there is a parallel phenomenon that occurs in language development in humans. Dr. Curtiss believes the brain is unable to construct a fully developed cognitive system to process language after puberty. Her research also indicates this affects some aspects of language learning, such as pronunciation or the acquisition of more complex syntactic structures (grammar), more than others.

For instance, the degree to which one is able to develop native-like pronunciation seems to be strongly affected by one's age at exposure to a language. The exact relationship between the ability to perceive sounds and the ability to produce them is not completely clear; however, research on accent in second language learners indicates that the younger one is when exposed to a new language, the more likely one is to eventually have native or near-native pronunciation.

There is extensive research showing that infants begin narrowing their focus to sounds relevant in their native language at a very early age. For example, Patricia Kuhl and her colleagues at the University of Washington, observing the reaction of infants to different sounds, have demonstrated that by six months, infants are tuning in to the sounds of their own language. By ten to twelve months they are not distinguishing sound differences that are meaningless in their language, but distinctive in others. Japanese infants, for example, no longer react to the difference between /r/ and /l/, significant in English, but not in Japanese.

Mapping Language in the Brain

It is now possible to use MRI technology to locate where in the brain activity is taking place when a person is engaged in certain tasks. By mapping increased blood flow in areas where neural activity occurs when a person uses a particular language, for instance, researchers can see where in the brain the language is processed.

Children's Language Acquisition

12 At the Memorial Sloan-Kettering Cancer Center in New York City, researchers have found that adults who learned two languages as young children used overlapping areas in the brain for processing their languages. Adults who learned a second language as teenagers or adults used more widely separated parts of the brain for their two languages. Researchers at the University of Basel in Switzerland, also using MRI techniques, compared the language processing of early and late bilinguals with similar results. Early bilinguals, who had acquired their languages before age three, were found to use less widely dispersed areas in the brains for language processing than late bilinguals, who had acquired their second language after the age of nine.

This would indicate that early languages (learned from birth or early childhood) are processed differently in the brain than late languages. If Dr. Curtiss is correct in her theory that the brain is not capable of developing a normally functioning cognitive system after puberty, when we use a language learned later in life, we are relying on a separate cognitive system. This could explain why adult language learners do not usually achieve the same levels of ability as children.

As part of the same study at the University of Basel, researchers compared the processing by early and late bilinguals of third languages learned as teenagers or adults. Early bilinguals were found to be using some of the same areas of the brain for aspects of language processing in their third languages as they did for their first two languages. The late bilinguals again used a more widely dispersed area. In other words, the language processing systems of the early bilinguals were apparently flexible enough to be used for some functions of a third language learned later in life.

Does this mean that early bilinguals are likely to be more easily able to learn additional languages later? According to Professor Jim Cummins, students in French immersion school programs in Canada who enter school speaking English and a home language (not French) tend to perform better in French than their peers who spoke only English at entry. There is also a growing body of evidence that bilinguals have a better understanding of how language works and how to manipulate it than monolinguals do.

Chapter Six

One of the difficulties that researchers face in testing the Critical Period Hypothesis is that it is clearly unethical to deprive an infant or child of linguistic interaction in order to see what happens. Linguists have examined information from unusual situations, such as those involving deaf children whose hearing impairment was not diagnosed until relatively late, or those involving so-called "wild children." There are also some interesting historical anecdotes concerning deliberate experiments arranged by persons uninhibited by ethical concerns.

There are some fascinating, though apocryphal, tales of early experiments conducted in order to establish the first human language, or to see whether language was instinctive or learned in human beings. One of the earliest of these stories concerns Psammeticus I, who ruled Egypt from approximately 640 to 610 B.C. According to the Greek historian Herodotus, Psammeticus tried to determine the original human language by isolating infants in the care of shepherds, who were under strict orders not to speak to them or allow them to be exposed to language in any way. Psammeticus believed that, in the absence of hearing other languages, the children would spontaneously speak the first human language. (According to Herodotus, their first word was "bekos," "bread" in Phrygian.)

Another story concerns King Frederick II of Sicily (1296-1337) who was reportedly inspired by Psammeticus's early experiment to conduct his own investigations. Unfortunately, all of the infants involved died, as the king's method was to simply leave them in the wild to fend for themselves.

Mogul Emperor Akbar the Great (1542-1605) had twenty to thirty infants raised in a silent house, called the Gung Mahal, with reasonable care, their only deprivation having been that of language. There are differing reports regarding Akbar's motivation. Some accounts indicate that he believed the children would not develop language without input and wanted to demonstrate this. Other accounts state he, too, hoped they would demonstrate an "original" human language. When the children were brought out of the Gung Mahal, after four years (or twelve, depending on the version of the story), they reportedly did not speak, although they may have used some signs.

Children's Language Acquisition

When Dr. Rachel Mayberry at McGill University in Montreal compared the proficiency in American Sign Language of deaf people who had learned the language at different ages, she found late learners were more likely to make errors in grammar and in the form of the sign, that is, the shape of the hand. In a short report in the May 2002 journal *Nature*, Dr. Mayberry along with colleagues Elizabeth Lock and Hena Kazmi report on their study of those who received little or no language exposure early in life to those who did, either through deaf parents who signed or because they became deaf after early childhood and hence had learned a spoken language. In addition to comparing proficiency for the two groups in tests of American Sign Language, the researchers also compared the two groups performance in learning a new language as adults. Those who hadn't been able to acquire a language in early childhood, due to not being able to hear the language being used around them and no opportunity to learn a sign language, didn't seem to process language as well as those who had been able to acquire a language early. They didn't perform as well in American Sign Language, nor were they able to learn new languages as easily.

Wild Children

Other support for the Critical Period Hypothesis comes from the information gathered on cases of "wild children," who spent their childhood in extreme conditions and were not socialized or exposed to language. Fortunately, cases of 'wild children' are relatively rare. Historical cases, such as that of Victor, discovered in France in 1799, have been examined by those interested in language development for clues as to the relative impact of nature vs. nurture on human language, as well as evidence for a critical period for language development. It has been difficult to draw conclusions from these cases, however, because such information as existed was recorded in unsystematic ways, and the influence of other factors such as malnutrition or the lack of opportunity for normal emotional development was unknown.

Chapter Six

The discovery of a modern day 'wild child' in California in 1970 caused a stir, and an attempt to combine research with treatment for the child resulted in controversy. Genie is the pseudonym given to the child for research and publication purposes. She had been kept in isolation by her parents in conditions of extreme neglect and deprivation for over ten years. Her progress in language development was studied after her discovery as part of the Genie Project.

According to Dr. Susan Curtiss, the primary investigator for the language component of the Genie Project, Genie was able to learn to communicate to some degree, and successfully acquired new vocabulary. However, by the time the study had ended, she still wasn't using grammatical sentences, an outcome that supports the theory that a critical period for language development does exist.

It is difficult to arrive at concrete conclusions from a case like Genie's. There is some evidence to indicate that Genie may have had some cognitive abnormalities not related to her mistreatment and isolation. Research on Genie ended in the mid 1970s amid accusations that attempts by some researchers to combine research and treatment had resulted in bad science and exploitation of the subject.

For those interested in further information on Genie, or other "wild children," Genie: A Scientific Tragedy, Russ Rymer, Harper Perennial, is a well written, highly critical account of the Genie case based on a series of articles originally published in **The New Yorker** magazine. Dr. Curtiss, one of the few researchers involved in the project to escape scathing criticism regarding her involvement with Genie, published an academic study entitled Genie: A Psycholinguistic Study of a Modern-Day 'Wild Child', Academic Press, currently out of print, but available through libraries. Another book of interest is Roger Shattuck's The Forbidden Experiment: The Story of the Wild Boy of Aveyron. Francois Truffaut's 1969 film **The Wild Child (L' Enfant sauvage)** is based on the same story.

Chapter Seven

Language Development Milestones

Language is a living thing.
—Gilbert Highet

For parents raising children bilingually, their children's language development can provoke anxiety. Maybe their child is mixing languages. Maybe he's not speaking one of them. Maybe he's not speaking either language and little David down the street was talking well before the same age. Advice can range from a reassuring, "Bilingual kids always talk late," to "You're confusing him." Even parents who hear more positive messages may worry. What if bilingualism isn't the reason their child isn't talking? What if there is some other reason? What if they don't do testing because they assume bilingual language acquisition is just taking more time, and there really is something wrong?

Chapter Seven

The table that follows describes how children are typically using language at different stages during the first four years of life. These language development milestones are based on information gathered from a number of sources, including interviews with professional speech and language specialists working with preschool and elementary school age children, and the American Academy of Pediatrics. Because children become bilingual in so many different ways and under such a variety of circumstances, the milestones for healthy language development on based on what is typical for monolingual children.

Typical Language Development

0 to 3 months

Infants seem to respond to familiar voices from birth. They startle in response to loud sounds. Parents may notice that their baby's crying sounds different depending on what the baby needs. Infants are generally cooing and making other vowel sounds by around two or three months of age.

3 to 6 months

New noises will catch babies' attention at this age. At about four months babies expand their own repertoire of sounds, adding consonants. By six months, babies are usually babbling, putting together vowel and consonant sounds, and stringing together syllables, i.e. "baba" "mama."

6 to 12 months

Infants begin to respond to their name during this period. At around nine months, a baby's babbling may begin to sound like real words. This is due in part to the fact that they are starting to use intonation. Infants are also likely to use sound to get others' attention, by shouting or shrieking. They understand and respond to words for familiar objects and people, and often the word, "no." Many infants start using their first word between eight and twelve months, but for some children the first word comes after twelve months.

Language Development Milestones

12 to 24 months

Between twelve and twenty-four months children are busily acquiring new vocabulary. Children at this age will generally respond to simple commands, and often repeat words or sounds heard in conversation, sometimes over and over again. Around age two some children are putting two or three words together to make simple sentences, i.e. "More juice." "Kitty bye-bye." Children at this age can usually point to their head, their tummy, or other parts of the body when asked. They begin to understand and may ask their own questions using words like "what" and "where."

24 to 36 months

Somewhere between the ages of two and three, many children experience an explosive growth in vocabulary. They are able to use descriptive words like 'big' and 'little,' as well as words describing their own state of being, such as 'hungry,' 'thirsty,' or 'tired.' Most children can respond appropriately to two stage commands, i.e. "Pick up the cup and put it on the table." Children's speech is becoming clearer. Parents and other family members understand what children are saying most of the time.

3 to 4 years

Children at this age are using four or more words in a sentence, and have both the vocabulary and grammar to participate in conversations about their day, or a story. People who don't know the child can usually understand most of what they say.

Chapter Seven

Parents should keep in mind that there is range in how closely individual children's development will follow this timetable. Some children simply develop more slowly than others. Some may be lagging in language development because their energy is focused on another area, such as motor skills. Children whose needs are met without much effort on their part may speak later. This can happen with younger siblings, who benefit from their older brothers and sisters' requests from adults.

How do parents know when they should be concerned? The following checklist is based on information provided by the Hanen Centre, a Canadian non-profit organization concerned with children's speech and language development. Even if your child is not showing some of the behaviors on the checklist, there may not be any real problem. These are simply indicators that language and related cognitive development are progressing normally. There are people, both bilingual and monolingual, who begin speaking quite late as children and later experience no problems. Some late talkers show exceptional spatial or mathematical abilities. Well-known late talkers include Albert Einstein, Benito Mussolini, mathematicians Julia Robinson and Ramanujan, and pianists Arthur Rubinstein and Clara Schumann.

An absence of the behaviors in the following list of questions is merely a sign that testing your child for hearing impairment or developmental issues would be wise. If you have concerns after going through the checklist, the place to start is with your child's general medical practitioner.

At three months, does your baby...

- startle at sudden sounds?

- turn toward a sound?

- show interest when you talk to him or her?

- make cooing (vowel) sounds?

Language Development Milestones

At six months, does your baby...

- use noise to try to get your attention?

- smile and make noise when you talk and smile?

At nine months, does your baby...

- reach out to be picked up?

- respond to his or her name?

- respond to "no"?

- babble?

At one year, does your baby...

- try to communicate using sounds and gestures?

- respond to simple phrases, i.e. "Come here"?

- play games like "peek-a-boo"?

At fifteen months, does your child...

- use one or two words?

- understand simple questions, i.e. "Where's the doggie?"

- repeat words others say?

- use intonation so that it sounds like the child is having conversations, even if though he or she doesn't use real words?

At eighteen months, does your child...

- use about ten words?

- use the word "no"?

- use the names of familiar objects and people, i.e. book, car, juice, Mommy, Daddy?

- answer the question, "What's this?" at least some of the time?

- usually look at you when trying to communicate?

Chapter Seven

At two years, does your child...

- enjoy hearing short, simple stories?

- use two word sentences?

- point to some body parts when asked?

- sometimes initiate conversation?

- ask short questions?

At three years, does your child...

- respond appropriately to a two part command? (i.e. "Pick up the ball and bring it here.")

- ask "why?" questions?

- talk about something that happened earlier in the day?

- use sentences of at least three words?

At four years, does your child...

- tell a story that you can understand either about a real experience or something imaginary?

- ask a lot of questions?

- stay on topic during a short conversation most of the time?

- talk during pretend play?

- use language to explain or create a pretend play situations with other children or caregivers?

At five years old, is your child...

- easy for most people outside the immediate family to understand when speaking?

- talking about things that happened in the past, future possibilities, and imaginary events?

- using grammar that sounds fairly 'adult'?

Language Development Milestones

13 # Differences in children's bilingual and mono-lingual language acquisition

Research indicates that children who grow up bilingual begin to speak, on average, later than monolingual peers do. This doesn't necessarily mean that children have more difficulty growing up speaking two languages rather than one, only that the process of learning two "native" languages takes more time. One reason for this could be that children require a certain amount of input and opportunity to interact in a language. It may take more time for bilingual children to reach the required level of language experience in each of their two languages than for a monolingual child to reach the same level in one. Bilingual children (and bilingual families) don't have any more time in the day than monolingual children do, but they are covering more linguistic ground. On the other hand, some bilingual children do begin speaking as early as the average monolingual child, some even earlier.

Children may also have a smaller vocabulary in each of their two languages than their monolingual peers. This is often true of adult bilinguals as well. On the other hand, if one were to count all of the words a bilingual knows in both languages, the total would probably be higher than that the number of words a monolingual speakers knows in his or her one. This is because a bilingual tends to use his or her languages in situation-specific ways. For example, a bilingual girl who goes to soccer matches and does yard work with her Spanish-speaking father may be able to talk about those topics in Spanish more easily than in English, the language she uses to talk about school. (Of course, if she plays soccer at school, there will be some overlap!)

When children first begin speaking, they will mix the two languages. This seems to be a normal part of the process of bilingual language acquisition. After a time, children work out the rules for which language they are supposed to speak to whom, and don't seem to experience problems differentiating between the two. When parents have some kind of pattern of language use, children quickly identify what the pattern is, and generally comply with it. Many parents have stories about children who were outraged upon first hearing a parent speak the "wrong" language, or upon being presented with a book of a favorite character in Dutch, for instance, in an English translation.

Chapter Seven

Mixing, or switching back and forth between two languages in a sentence or conversation, is known as 'code-switching.' If the adults in the household do a lot of code-switching, children are likely to do the same. This can hinder development in both languages, but especially the home language. This is because the child is more likely to encounter monolingual speakers of the community dominant language, at school and elsewhere, and will quickly learn that code-switching is not appropriate in speaking with them.

Young children will often use one word from one language in a sentence in the other. Later, children code-switch using similar strategies as adults do, for instance, changing language in response to the subject or emotional tenor of the conversation, or as a way of redirecting or calling for someone's attention. Mixing languages within a single word is more unusual, but especially with some sort of compound word, is possible. Again, this is less likely to continue if the boundaries of his or her languages are clear.

For some families code-switching can be a kind of game, or just a family language style. If children have plenty of opportunities to use their languages outside the immediate family, this is not a problem. On the other hand, if input in one of the languages is limited, parents may want to strive for more consistency.

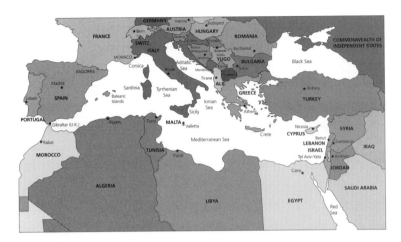

Chapter Eight

The Affective Dimension: Personality, Temperament and Emotional Issues

After all, when you come right down to it, how many people speak the same language even when they speak the same language?
—**Russell Hoban**

The role emotion and personality play in the acquisition of languages has been the subject of limited research. The factors frequently studied include motivation, anxiety, self-confidence and other characteristics that affect a person's attitude toward learning. Some experts would discount such affective factors in the case of childhood language learning, while others believe they can have an impact on children's experiences and ultimate proficiency

Chapter Eight

in two languages. As a parent, it is hard not to believe that your child's personality doesn't play a role in how they learn languages, just as it seems to impact how they approach everything else, from walking to the first day of kindergarten to preparing for their university entrance exams.

Temperament and learning styles can affect how children learn best and this may have implications for how parents can most effectively create a language environment that facilitates their children's acquisition of two languages. It makes sense to work to put your child in a situation where they can use their strengths, as well as improve on their weaknesses.

The degree to which a parent and child's temperaments are a good fit together may have an impact on how well the child learns two languages, too, as well as on the level of tension in the family associated with language, especially the minority language. Parents often experience frustration when their children react to things in unexpected ways, or reject a strategy that works well for the parent.

Parents in bilingual families are sometimes surprised by the emotional reactions they themselves have in response to various developments in the family regarding language use, especially by the intensity of such feelings. Parents can also find themselves in conflict with each other over language issues. Even when they agree on the general aim of family bilingualism, disagreements are possible on a variety of things, such as what language strategy is best, choice of school, what to do when children are struggling with one of the languages, and how to deal with children's feelings or the reactions of relatives.

Children may also have strong feelings about language use in their family. When they understand a parent's language in a family in which only one parent speaks the minority language, this can create a special tie between parent and child, something that children may value as much as the parent. It can also cause some children discomfort. They feel a sense of separation from the other parent who speaks only the majority language, or are concerned that that parent is being left out. Speaking a minority language in the family can be a source of pride for children, and help foster an interest in

The Affective Dimension

their heritage. For others, however, it can also raise fears of being too different from other children, or of having friends think their parents are weird. When being part of a bilingual family is treated as something ordinary by the parents, extreme emotional reactions from everyone are less likely.

Personality as factor in learning languages

Does personality determine how good people are at learning languages? Even shy, stubborn babies eventually learn their first language, but parents often feel when it comes to a second language, their children's personality and temperament has a significant impact on their language development. In an optimum situation, personality should not be much of an issue. When people need languages, they learn them. However, the majority of bilingual families in the United States find that it can be a struggle to maintain their family bilingualism, no matter whether their child is introverted, extroverted, high-strung or easy-going.

Research on second language acquisition in children by Professor Lily Wong Fillmore at the University of California at Berkeley demonstrates that, at least in the short-term, language learning outcomes can be affected by factors such as temperament or personality. In other words, a shy child who is being introduced to his second language at preschool may seemingly learn the language more slowly. One reason for this could be the child is interacting less with his classmates, which gives him fewer opportunities to practice and less motivation to learn the language. On the other hand, there is also research indicating that in the long term, an introvert who continues to have contact with the language is no less likely to achieve mastery of a new language than an extrovert. The strengths and weaknesses these personalities bring to the task are simply different.

Children may succeed with language in different ways, and a shy child, who tends to monitor himself carefully, may use more accurate grammar than his siblings even in his weaker language. If he has a good ear, his pronunciation may be more like a native speaker, too. More introverted children also have the potential to become strong readers and writers in both languages.

Chapter Eight

On the other hand, a shy child may have more trouble expressing himself in his weaker language, simply because he hasn't had as much practice in doing so as a more extroverted child.

An outgoing, bubbly personality may initially learn more quickly, speaking more fluently, with a larger vocabulary, and may feel at home in more social situations. An extroverted child's strong desire to interact and communicate with others can help him develop bilingual language skills if he needs both languages to talk with people. The same child may be careless in his grammar, however, or have a non-native accent that persists, even with correction from others, because he is primarily motivated in communication rather than accuracy.

Temperament

There are a number of different theories of temperament, from Myers-Briggs test types to color-coding of personalities. The value to parents may lie less in the particular theory than the idea that children come with some inborn characteristics. It can be reassuring to know that something your child does that drives you crazy is absolutely normal, and that your reaction to it is normal as well. When things are not going well in the area of language, some parents find it helpful to use a systematic approach that depersonalizes the conflicts that may arise in the family. This sort of approach doesn't work for everyone, but it can be useful for those who enjoy learning about child development, family dynamics, or popular psychology.

Dr. William Carey, author of the book <u>Understanding Your Child's Temperament</u>, has developed a way of thinking about temperament based on nine traits: intensity, persistence, sensitivity, perceptiveness, adaptability, regularity, energy, initial reaction, and mood. According to Dr. Carey, every child falls somewhere along a continuum with regard to each characteristic, as does every parent. A seven-year-old who is high on the persistence scale might spend most of a weekend absorbed in a project such as building a Lego city. A two-year-old high in both persistence and intensity may have tantrums that go on for hours.

The Affective Dimension

Where one falls on the scale for each of the traits doesn't have any inherent implications for how well we are likely to learn languages overall. However, it may have some effect on how we react to these traits under certain conditions, and maybe even indicate in what areas of language we might excel. Understanding your children's temperaments can help parents understand why one strategy for language is working well with one child, but not the other. It can reduce incidents of blaming, which may relieve tension or anxiety regarding language learning in general.

If you are starting off with two languages from birth, at first it is merely a matter of providing as much consistent exposure to both languages as you can, no matter what the baby's temperament or personality seems to be. Some aspects of a baby's personality may be obvious from day one, but in the beginning most babies eat, sleep and cry. It takes parents awhile to figure out where a child might be on the adaptability scale, for instance, but as children get older, personality and preferences begin to reveal themselves. A parent's ability to work with the child's personality and temperament can become a valuable tool.

Another important idea in thinking about temperament is 'goodness of fit' between parents and children. Parents may assume their children will react in a similar way as themselves to certain situations. Even after realizing this isn't always the case, the child's behavior may be hard for the parent to understand and can even cause them to get angry.

For example, an easy-going, extroverted, stay-at-home parent may see a language playgroup as being a good opportunity for their child to interact with other children who use the same language. The parent herself may enjoy chatting with other parents, and find the social aspect of the playgroup a relief from the quiet, somewhat isolated experience of being home all day with a young child. If the child is more introverted, and perhaps highly sensitive to environmental factors like noise, he may be overwhelmed by the crowded, noisy gym where the playgroup meets, and become clingy and unhappy. Especially if his mother becomes angry, the child starts to associate the language with a negative experience. If the parent understands the problem, she can take some steps to make her child more comfortable. Maybe

Chapter Eight

she could ask another parent from the playgroup to meet her at the park instead so the children could play. At the very least, she can plan on arriving early, before the gym is crowded and leave early.

Learning style approaches to language

Some parents may prefer to use a learning styles approach to helping their children learn languages, rather than an approach that focuses on temperament or personality. Information on learning styles is useful for parents who are planning to do more formal work on the language at home, teaching the child to read, for instance.

A popular example of learning style theory is Howard Gardner's theory of multiple intelligences, which assumes that each person has preferred ways of learning.

Gardner identified seven different types of intelligence: linguistic; logical/mathematical; musical; spatial; bodily kinesthetic; interpersonal; and intrapersonal. More recently he has added an understanding of the natural world to the list. In the United States, education usually focuses primarily on linguistic and logical/mathematical intelligence. Bilingual parents are often language-oriented learners, and may be either more visually or aurally inclined.

The Affective Dimension

Four Common Learning Styles

- **Linguistic learners** are the children whose teachers rave about their strong verbal skills. They like stories and jokes, and often are good readers, although some may prefer to take in information aurally.

- **Spatial-visual learners** often enjoy drawing, puzzles, and building toys like Legos or K'nex. They may be very interested in machines and sometimes need to see things graphically in order to understand and/or remember them.

- **Kinetic learners** need to move. They like to feel and touch, and may want to show rather than tell. Hands-on learning works best. Kinetic learners working on literacy skills may like to copy or write down information or a story. They may be interested in letters, characters or objects they can see, feel and touch.

- **Logical learners** like to figure out how things work. They often enjoy puzzles and math. Patterns and relationships are interesting to logical learners and games involving rhyming patterns, or looking for shapes of letters of characters inspire them.

It is important to structure your child's environment as best you can, so that you set him up to succeed. An understanding of temperament or learning style can be helpful for parents attempting to plan family life in a way that will help their children learn two languages, especially if they are planning to take on the additional task of teaching the children to read and write in both languages. The important thing to remember about temperament or personality issues is all children can successfully learn two (or more) languages. However, the way your child learns best may not be the way you prefer.

Chapter Eight

Some useful books on parenting, temperament and learning style include:

- <u>Understanding Your Child's Temperament</u> by Dr. William Carey and the Children's Hospital of Philadelphia. Published by: Hungry Minds, Inc.

- <u>Frames of Mind: The Theory of Multiple Intelligences</u> by Howard Gardner. Published by: Basic Books.

- <u>Kids, Parents and Power Struggles</u> and <u>Raising Your Spirited Child</u> by Mary Sheedy Kurcinka. Published by: HarperCollins.

- <u>A Mind at a Time</u> by Mel Levine. Published by: Simon & Schuster.

- <u>Temperament Tools: Working with Your Child's Inborn Traits</u> by Helen Neville and Diane Clark Johnson. Published by: Parenting Press, Inc.

Emotional issues for parents in bilingual families

Some parents discover their own experience in the family's minority language and culture is more limited than they had previously realized, because they left their home country at an early age, or before they had had certain life experiences. This discovery can be disconcerting. The language(s) a person speaks makes up a part of one's sense of identity, and to find that one has gaps or shortcomings in a language toward which one had felt a sense of full ownership is distressing and often shocking. Others, of course, may find this amusing, and enjoy learning how to fill in those gaps in their knowledge of their own language and culture.

People who had thought up until having children they had settled in another country primarily due to circumstances in educational choice, employment, or in deference to their partner's wishes, may realize there were characteristics of their own culture they didn't find attractive and that the opportunity to leave those things behind played a larger role in their decision than they realized. Many cultures require a degree of deference to authority, especially from children, that can clash with typical American styles of childrearing.

The Affective Dimension

Other areas that can be problematic include gender role expectations and religious practice. Finding ways to avoid those particular aspects of the culture can be a challenge when trying to teach children the language, especially as extended family members holding those values are often an important source minority language interaction for children in bilingual families.

For some parents, making a conscious effort to teach their children their minority language brings up unresolved feelings about having left home or the home country. Parents may realize how far away they are from other family members and find themselves wishing for closer connections with relatives back home. When closer ties can be achieved, these can contribute significantly to children's success in acquiring languages, and parents may derive satisfaction from these strengthened ties, too. On the other hand, when financial circumstances, geographic distance, or political conflicts prevent frequent visits or contact, the lack of interaction with people back home can be a real frustration and a source of unhappiness for parents.

Sometimes immigrant parents don't feel as though they completely belong to either country. Often without even realizing it, parents in this situation may be ambivalent about the degree to which they want their child to identify with their minority language and culture because they don't want their children to also experience that sense of not belonging. This can lead the parent to be less supportive of their children's development in the minority language, even when they consciously believe they want their children to learn it.

Mehdi found that many of the books, music, and other materials he obtained for his daughter in special shops or on trips back home didn't express values he would otherwise choose to share with her. He also felt uncomfortable about the idea of initiating and continuing friendships primarily for the sake of supporting his daughter's language development.

At the other end of the spectrum, some parents are angry when their children don't have the same level of appreciation their parents have of the minority language. They may push too hard, or find themselves reacting negatively to their child's interests in the majority language and culture, and this can result in language becoming a source of tension in the household.

Chapter Eight

Speakers of indigenous languages may also be ambivalent about their children learning their minority language because they may associate the language with being marginalized socially, politically, and economically. In some cases, indigenous languages are learned primarily at school because of a generation gap between proficient speakers of the language. Parents who don't speak their minority language well themselves may not know how to best promote their children's achievement in the language. They may also be more concerned about how well their children are doing in other areas academically, viewing those subjects as being more important to their children's opportunities for success later in life. Even when the school supports children's learning of indigenous languages, children pick up on their parents' feelings.

Dr. Evangeline Parsons-Yazzie, professor of Navajo at Northern Arizona University explains: "Children need to believe their language is just as important and has the same status as the English language in order to want it. For years, American Indians have been told their language, culture, lifestyle, and traditions were not good enough and now our children believe it. My message has been, 'Let us glamorize our indigenous languages and motivate our children to honor them and it will go further and be used just as much as English.'"

Jessi Koeffler admits that while one of the reasons for her family's decision to de-emphasize the use of German at home was because the family felt it important to have a sense of belonging in the community where they lived, a down-side to this decision is that her husband sometimes feels like a bit of an outsider, even in his own family. At his work he is subject to a good deal of well-intentioned ribbing about stereotypically German traits such as efficiency, and he is also aware his accent marks him as a non-native in the United States. One night at dinner, his eldest was entertaining the family with a dead-on imitation of her father's accent and speaking style when she caught sight of his face and realized she had hurt his feelings.

"We had all been laughing," says Jessi. "It was very funny, but then I saw his expression and realized he was thinking, 'Even in my own family!'"

The Affective Dimension

Special Family Roles for Minority Languages

The family's minority language may be the one the family uses for nicknames, teasing and endearments. Parents may not realize how often they switch to their own native language when they are angry. My husband has been known in moments of frustration to call our daughter something that roughly translates as 'small poisonous snake.' This can obviously set up negative associations with the minority language.

'Mixed' Marriages

A monolingual parent who speaks the country's majority language, married to someone who speaks two languages, may like the idea of the children becoming bilingual, too. However, the amount of effort that parent makes to support the project can vary considerably. For example, the extent of his or her enthusiasm for extended visits to the home country of the family's minority language may depend on how well that parent gets along with his or her in-laws, especially if the trips require significant financial sacrifices for the family. Choosing a school based on the availability of a language program may be less acceptable to that parent, especially if the burden of extra driving time or volunteering at the school will fall mostly on that parent's shoulders. The monolingual parent may be less willing to insist that reluctant children continue to attend Saturday school or other activities where exposure to the minority language is the main reason for going.

On the other hand, sometimes the parent who doesn't speak the minority language is more enthusiastic than the native-speaking parent about the children learning the language. Unfortunately, it is the parent who speaks the minority language who must make most of the effort to provide children with opportunities to speak. When the bilingual parent is perfectly comfortable in the majority language, and when the minority language plays a limited role in the family's life, he or she may find it difficult to keep up use of it with the children.

Chapter Eight

Even when parents are using two languages from birth, the children's development in one language, usually the majority language, typically progresses more quickly than the other. Parents may feel anxious about this unequal development and the parent who speaks the language in which the child has less proficiency may end up feeling less able to communicate and distanced from the child.

When families in which only one parent speaks the minority language decide to bring up the children using both languages, the parent who speaks the majority language may decide to learn it, too. This is a good way to show support for the other parent's language and can help to promote a feeling of family unity. Sometimes parents have conflicts on this issue, when the parent with the minority language feels the other parent isn't trying very hard to learn, underestimates the effort required, or simply isn't helpful as a teacher. Majority language parents may find they do better by finding a class, or someone else to act as a tutor, rather than relying on their spouse to teach them the language.

According to the British Council, the UK's international organization for international and cultural relations, a study of bilingual families in Wales demonstrates that 92% of children in families with two Welsh-speaking parents will also speak Welsh. In homes where only one parent speaks Welsh, children are much less likely to speak it, with only 49% of the children with a Welsh-speaking father reported to speak Welsh and 54% of those with a mother who spoke Welsh. Clearly, it helps when both parents speak the language.

Accents

Parental reaction to hearing their child speaking the family's minority language with a non-native accent can range from amusement to horror. This is a good time to bring out the poker face. Unless your child is trying to be funny, he probably won't appreciate being laughed at, and if you are visibly upset or concerned about the accent your child may try to avoid speaking the language altogether. Sometimes parents or other family members will tease the children a little about their accent. This can make children self-conscious and is probably not a good idea.

The Affective Dimension

Why does it matter when a child speaks the language with an accent? For some parents, it actually doesn't. For others, it is a constant reminder of a gap in the experience of the minority language and culture their children are having, or an intrusion of the majority language and culture. There are parents who feel that when their child speaks with an accent in the minority language, this means they have failed to some degree in their efforts to bring up the child bilingually. It is important to have thought about what bilingualism means for you at the beginning and if you as a parent will be satisfied with nothing less than balanced bilingual skills, it is up to you to ensure that your child is in a situation that will enable him or her to acquire them.

Emotional Issues for Children

When parents have become quite assimilated in the country where they currently live, they may use their minority language primarily to stay in touch with old friends and relatives, and perhaps to keep up on current events back home. It can be disappointing for these parents when children are not very motivated to use the family's minority language, but this lack of motivation is understandable. After all, the children may not even know the people with whom parents use the language to communicate, and they are unlikely to be interested in the politics of a parent's 'home country'.

It can also take parents by surprise when their children resist certain aspects of language or language use. Language is not culture- or value-free, but we are often not consciously aware of everything our language use reflects. Children may be impatient with honorific styles, implied deference to authority, or rituals of greeting that are an automatic part of speaking the language.

Younger children are usually relatively free of the self-consciousness that inhibits adult language learners, who are concerned about making mistakes. This is an advantage as they develop their skills because they don't worry so much about getting things wrong or about the reactions of other people. Once children begin to worry about fitting in with their peers, they may be reluctant to speak the language, at least in public. Families sometimes find at this point the children will use the family's minority language with a parent who speaks it as a native-speaker, but don't want to with a parent who speaks the language well, but not natively.

Chapter Eight

Children who believe they are speaking the language well are more likely to continue with enthusiasm, so even if they are over-estimating their abilities in the language, confidence is a good thing. For older children, discovering they are not as proficient as they had thought can serve to motivate them to work harder, but it will depend on how valuable they perceive the language to be. For some children, finding out they do not sound like native speakers of their minority language can be a real setback, and discourage them from persisting with the language.

Children make strong associations between people and languages. Parents who want to instill a firm habit of use of a certain language in particular contexts or with certain people sometimes use strategies that seem a little extreme to outsiders, like pretending to their children they don't speak the majority language at all. This can be quite effective, though, and depending on the languages used in the family's social circle, children may believe it for a long time. I have heard of children informing monolingual teachers or other adults that there isn't any use trying to talk to the parent because he or she doesn't understand the majority language, or of parents announcing that the new baby only speaks the minority language, thereby successfully promoting its use between siblings.

As a result of young children's association of a parent with a particular language, they may become upset when parents change languages. To the child, the parent may sound unnatural when speaking a language children are not used to hearing from them. Especially if parents are native bilinguals, they may take on changes in pitch or body language when they change language. Many bilinguals feel that some aspects of their personality change when they switch languages, and this can be unsettling for children. Parents using a family language they don't speak as well can seem diminished in children's eyes. For instance, my daughter's attitude when pointing out my mistakes in Farsi seems to alternate between glee and embarrassment, and she currently refuses to allow her father to read aloud to her in English at all.

Chapter Nine

Examining Motivations and Setting Goals

Language exerts hidden power, like the moon on the tides.
— **Rita Mae Brown**

Generally speaking, we are more likely to succeed when we know what we want. Imagine your child in two languages; what do you see? Is he comfortably moving back and forth between a close-knit minority language community of extended family and friends and the majority language community? Is she dazzling others with her linguistic talents? Is he happily spending summer at grandma's house in the home country of your family's minority language? Staying in touch with cousins there? Maybe he or she is studying in the home country of the family's minority language for a year or two.

Chapter Nine

How about as an adult? Is your grown-up child an active member of your ethnic language community? Perhaps with bilingual skills, she is making a special contribution as a teacher or in the medical profession. Maybe he is a sophisticated world traveler, with educational opportunities not available to others. Perhaps she is raising bilingual children of her own.

I think it is important to be honest and recognize the fantasies most parents have about their kids. What are children if not possibility? Then, of course, we have to get realistic. If you actually feel that bilingual skills may give your child an advantage in educational or career opportunities, it may be well to remember that most kids are not thinking that far ahead. Also, they are going to have their own ideas about career goals, likely involving firemen, super-heroes, and ballerinas.

Different Motivations for Parents and Children

Children will not be motivated to learn their family's minority language because it may, in the future, lead to a fantastic scholarship, a high-powered business career, or even the ability to give back to their ethnic community. Until they are much older, they will not care that English is used globally, that the ability to speak a language like Arabic or Japanese is relatively rare and therefore valuable, or that being able to read and write in their minority language can greatly enhance employment opportunities. You may find any or all of these to be compelling motivations for trying to raise a bilingual child, but they are your motivations, not your child's.

> "Yes, I want my son to speak Spanish. But I think it is my responsibility to speak English, too. I think he can accept the Spanish more if it's not like a box that I am stuck inside."
>
> **—Bernarda Aquilar, USA**

Examining Motivations and Setting Goals

Children are also unlikely to want to learn a language so that parents can show off their skills to friends and family. (In fact, asking children to perform is probably going to have exactly the opposite effect.) Nor will they be at all motivated to learn because parents believe they will reap cognitive benefits such as more flexible problem solving skills, an improved ability to learn languages in the future, or higher scores on standardized tests. Again, those are the parents' ideas.

> "[My youngest brother] has big chances, more than the rest of us, but he doesn't care. He just plays, wants to watch TV."
>
> **—Charlie Lam, USA**

Perhaps you feel that knowing the language is an important part of understanding your culture and heritage. Maybe you are concerned that, without speaking the language, your child will be even more distanced from family members far away. This may be true, but it is also true that although speaking the language can foster these family and cultural connections, the connections are important to fostering the development of language skills. It works both ways. Children are more likely to want to use a language they need to speak with people they love rather than learn a language so they can talk with distant relatives they've only met on the phone.

We invest a lot in our children, and letting go can be hard. Separating your own desires and reasons for deciding on raising bilingual children, and your children's likely motivations for learning two languages is important because they won't be the same. This means what works to motivate you won't necessarily motivate your children, and when you start mapping out a strategy for bilingual family life, you have to imagine things from their point of view. If you are going to succeed, you will have recognized your own motivations for taking on the project, and realized that your children's motivations for going along with it will be entirely different.

Chapter Nine

It's easier to stay motivated if you know where you are going and what steps you're taking to get there. Breaking a hypothetical bilingual family lifestyle down into concrete steps, plans and strategies helps parents to know whether or not they are staying on track. You will be more likely to realize that you are using English at dinner if you make a commitment to only using the family's minority language. If you plan to make a trip to visit relatives in Denmark, Mexico, or Puerto Rico every other summer, you'll notice if you don't go.

Dream for Your Children; Set Goals for Yourself

Parents have to remember that although they have a long-term vision with regard to their children's ability to speak two languages, the goals they have in mind should be things the parents can accomplish, not the children. You have to set specific goals for yourself in order to create a language-rich environment, give them opportunities to use the minority language, and encourage positive feelings toward their minority language and culture. You can't force your children to acquire the language.

To make an analogy, most parents realize that choosing a profession for their children doesn't work very well. Deciding that your son or daughter will become a doctor may be a prescription of misery for your child. On the other hand, ensuring that your child has the chance for a well-rounded education so if the child does take advantage of it, he or she will have the smarts and the knowledge to pursue medicine (or teaching, or documentary film-making) as a career; that's excellent parenting.

> "The opportunity was there, it just didn't make sense to waste it. There were times when it felt silly and I thought, 'What am I doing?' Having the school available was great. I don't know if I would have continued without that."
>
> **—Leslie Tucker, USA**

Examining Motivations and Setting Goals

It doesn't make sense to set concrete goals like my child will have a vocabulary of at least 10 words in both languages by 30 months. You don't have any control over that. Maybe your child won't talk at all until he's three. On the other hand, you can commit yourself to reading to your child in one language or the other, or both, depending on your language strategy, every day. You can decide that you will only speak your family's minority language with your child. You can make a commitment to arranging your child's schedule so that he hears the minority language at least 50% of the time. You can commit to traveling with your child to the home country where your family's minority language is spoken at least once a year, or once every three years; whatever you think is actually possible for your family. Then, in order to make that happen, you may need to consider setting some financial goals as well.

It is also necessary to think about how, with the resources available, you can achieve a certain goal such as having your child in a minority language environment at least 50% of the time. When families break a goal like this into smaller action steps, they will be doing different things. In one family, this could involve one parent leaving paid employment in order to provide the children with more time in the family's minority language. Another family may decide to fix up a guest room to make it easier for extended family to visit. Another may look for a childcare provider who speaks the family's minority language.

Chapter Nine

Accepting the Limitations of Your Language Situation

You are going to be more satisfied with your children's progress in two languages if your expectations are realistic, given the unique language situation of your own family. You can only make the best of the situation that you have. Being honest with yourself about the amount of exposure you will be able to give your child to the language can save you some disappointment later on, or can enable you to make the changes you'll need to make to give your children more opportunities to use the minority language.

When Two Languages are a Necessity, not a Choice

One of the most common reasons for raising children bilingually is necessity. Parents who don't speak the majority language of the country where they live, families who live within two language communities, and those who travel frequently between two different countries may not have a choice regarding whether their children will grow up with one language or two. In this case, setting goals to ensure the children are getting enough exposure to each language may not be necessary. However, these families will still need to make important decisions that will influence how their children's bilingualism develops, such as whether it is important their children be literate in both languages, the degree of fluency in each language the family will aim for, and the steps the family will take to help children develop those skills.

> "If we had thought about it, maybe we would have started her with a different language, one that she would get a chance to use more. We just decided that she should learn my first language, but actually, between the two of us, her mom and I speak five languages. Maybe another would have made more sense."
>
> **—Mehdi, father of one, USA**

Examining Motivations and Setting Goals

For families who live in communities where there are many speakers of their minority language, setting goals that focus on literacy, rather than language in general, may be more important. Short-term goals might include researching resources available in your community for developing literacy in the language, including your local library, and finding a children's story hour in the language. Intermediate goals might include educating yourself on literacy development in children. Notice these are goals for the parent, not the child.

These families will also need to think about how they are going to maintain their children's minority language after the children start school. Even in communities where children could use their minority language, they may choose not to. Parents can talk to other families they know in the area, who possibly have similar language situations. Other families may be able to share ideas about what has worked to motivate their children to use the minority language, and also what they have tried that hasn't worked very well. Strategies range from paying for cable in order to watch TV in the minority language to sending children to visit their cousins in the home country where the family's minority language is spoken.

"I never used the language with them. They live here and I don't feel that Farsi is their language. Maybe if my husband had been interested, but he and I had always used English before, so that's really our family's language now."

—Darya, Iranian-American mother of two, USA

Chapter Nine

Family Ties and Cultural Identity

Is it important to you that your child is able to communicate with other family members in the minority language? Are there people with whom your child will be in contact who only speak the minority language? Another motivation for parents who decide to raise their children with two languages is to strengthen family ties or promote cultural identification.

Sometimes in families where only one parent speaks the family's minority language, that parent feels strongly that the child should learn the language. This can be a way of promoting family solidarity. It can also alleviate the parent's feeling of being an alien or outsider in his or her own family when the children feel a sense of connection to the minority language and culture. Sometimes when parents who are living in a different country than their own parents or extended family, they hope that a change to a more child-centered lifestyle will somehow bring the language of their childhood into more prominence in their life. It may happen, but without a specific plan it may not.

Examining Motivations and Setting Goals

Your Family's Language Resources

Before you start making plans, look around and see what kinds of resources you will have to draw on, and ask yourself honestly what kinds of changes in your family life you are willing to make in order to foster bilingual language skills for your children. Families sometimes find that, although their family bilingualism is important, other values win out on occasion.

It is fine to decide not to buy a house in a certain neighborhood just because there are quite a few speakers of your family's minority language who live there. For that matter, you may decide you want to live in a small town, where no one else speaks the language for miles. The important thing is to recognize that you are making a trade-off, so that you can make a decision about how, or even whether, you want to compensate for the loss of language support.

There are families who decide the effort required to raise bilingual children is not justified. That is a legitimate choice, too.

Chapter Nine

When Only One Parent Speaks the Minority Language

In marriages where only one person speaks the minority language, the couple uses the majority language to communicate with each other. This pattern can be highly resistant to change. The couple is accustomed to communicating at a certain level of depth and ease. When one person is struggling to acquire the language, it can be hard for both to give up actual communication just to facilitate that person's acquisition of the new language. Some couples find that it works fine for each parent to use a different language with the children, and the only problem is that because the couple uses the majority language together, the children tend to have less exposure to the minority language.

Sometimes two language couples that generally use the majority language together are surprised to discover how little the minority language is actually used in their life together. Although the parent who speaks the minority language may read a newspaper or go on-line to check the news in the minority language every day, and talk on the phone with friends or relatives several times a week, this level of exposure does not translate to their children.

It is important to think about these things ahead of time, so that you're not surprised when the children's language development is uneven. Sometimes when this happens, parents get discouraged and decide to give up. Even worse, children can pick up on their disappointment, and feel that they have failed. If your children are learning even a little of the family's minority language under conditions that are not conducive to acquiring it, they should be proud of that fact, and so should you. You certainly don't want them to be associating their minority language with failure. This can lead to negative feelings toward the culture of the minority language and even about learning languages in general.

Examining Motivations and Setting Goals

What Role does the Minority Language Play in Your Family Life?

Even if you think having a child is going to cause you to change your lifestyle in ways that will promote more use of the family's minority language, it is a good idea to think about the role your minority language plays in your life now. Remember having a child takes a lot of time and energy, and when we are under stress we tend to fall back on habits. Asking yourself the following questions will give you a sense of whether your child is likely to perceive the minority language as necessary to participate in family life, based on your current habits and practices. Then you will have a better idea of what kind of bilingualism you should be aiming for, and the magnitude of the lifestyle change you might need to make to best support your child's acquisition of two languages.

1. How often is my child likely to see speakers of the minority language outside the immediate household, especially monolingual speakers? Will any of these be children?

2. How often do we currently see family or friends, and use the minority language?

3. Is most of my contact with family and friends who speak the minority language in person, by phone, letter, or email?

4. How often do we participate in cultural or religious events and activities where the minority language is spoken? (Possibilities include attending religious services, holiday gatherings, sporting events, family picnics, etc.)

5. What language do my partner or spouse and I use most often together?

6. Do both my partner and I both speak the minority language?

7. At gatherings of friends or relatives who speak the minority language, what language do the children present seem to be using with one another most?

Chapter Nine

If the minority language does not play a major role currently in your daily life, what can you do? At this point most parents (or parents to be) decide to make their minority language more of a priority, but this resolve will not sustain itself without some careful thought and long-term planning.

What changes are you and your partner able and willing to make to give the minority language a more prominent role in your family life? In order to answer this question, you may need to think about why that language doesn't play a larger role now and what you can do about it.

Does only one parent speak the language? Will the parent who doesn't speak it learn it? Why or why not? Is there physical distance from other speakers of the language? Emotional distance? Consider your own attitudes toward assimilation in the country where you live now. How do you feel, in general, about others who speak your minority language who live in that country? Do you seek them out?

Arranging trips to visit relatives in the home country where the family's minority language is spoken is often a very successful way for families in the United States to give their children a boost in the language. Such trips are highly motivational, allowing children to experience the language in an immersion setting and the effects of the trip can last beyond the time period spent there because children are able make contacts with people outside the immediate family who speak their minority language. The longer the trip is the better.

Some families can easily arrange their lives so that they move back and forth between countries. For most of us, though, time and money are obstacles to this kind of lifestyle. For Americans it can be difficult to arrange such trips because, relative to many Europeans, Americans have short vacations. Although the children may be out of school all summer, one or both parents will probably be working all but a few weeks. Teachers and academics may have an advantage in terms of time in planning a trip abroad, at least during summer, although money may still be an issue. If there is a stay-at-home parent in the family, that person might take the children alone, even if it is to visit the other parent's family.

Examining Motivations and Setting Goals

If you are currently in a situation that doesn't allow for this kind of travel, would it be possible for one or both parents to change their work situation to allow for it? Is it possible to arrange for a sabbatical, a year or six month off from work? If your first child is an infant, or even just on the way, it is not too early to start thinking about how the family might spend a year abroad when the child is in kindergarten. Families of moderate circumstances might still be able to spend one or more years during their children's childhood living in the country where their minority language is spoken, but it may involve years of planning and saving.

Sometimes a trip to the home country isn't possible, due to political conflicts, instability or other reasons. When there are extended family members who also live abroad, either in the same country as you or another one, this is another option for a family trip that can promote bilingual language skills.

For some families, raising their children in the minority language and culture is important enough that they choose to move to a community where the language is better supported. This might mean moving to a bigger city, where there is an ethnic community of speakers of the minority language and schooling in the language available. It could also mean simply moving closer to other family members. Sometimes having extended family members come to stay with the family, or even live permanently, works out very well for everyone.

Chapter Nine

Deciding on a Pattern
for Family Language Use

At minimum, parents should decide on a pattern for family language use, even if they currently use the family's minority language most or all of the time. Some people make the mistake of assuming their children will acquire the language because the parents use it, but when the family lives in a monolingual environment, this is not necessarily true. Even if the children hear the language all the time at home, they may develop mostly receptive skills in the language, or may use it with a relatively limited vocabulary.

The most common patterns, described in Chapter 4, are one person—one language (OPOL) or home language-outside language. For minority language maintenance after the children start school, the home language approach may work best, but families have to consider the difficulties their children may experience if they don't know the majority language when they start school. The one person—one language strategy can alleviate that concern, but may be less successful in promoting bilingual skills when the person providing the minority language works and is not able to spend as much time with the children. Parents should make careful consideration of the other language resources the family will be able to draw on before making their decision on a language use pattern for the family.

NETHERLANDS, BELGIUM
& LUXEMBOURG

Chapter Ten

Choosing a School

He was so learned that he could name a horse in nine languages; so ignorant that he bought a cow to ride on.
—Benjamin Franklin

Choosing a school is an important decision for any family. Parents must decide which school will best fit their children, taking into account factors such as location, cost, school and class size, demographics, educational philosophy and methodology, special programs, and childcare needs. In addition, there are less tangible factors such as whether you share the values of the school community, or how you feel when you walk through the doors. Children do well when parent and school goals are in harmony.

"The schedule for the school year is different, so when they are in Japan during our vacation here, they can go to school for a few weeks. That's really good for them; they can see where they are in relation to their peers. It motivates them. The math is much harder there."

—Dr. Larry Kominz, Oregon

Chapter Ten

Bilingual families also need to determine what role the school will play in supporting their children's bilingual language development. If you can find one, you will want a school where the teachers value bilingualism, even if the school doesn't have any special language programs. Parents in bilingual families who are considering a school because of its language program(s) will want to make sure they've thought about the school as a whole, not just the fact that it offers a language program. Choices

Before investigating schools, it is a good idea to know what you are looking for. Questions like the following can serve as a starting point:

- Would I prefer a public or private school?
- Would I prefer a small or large school?
- How important is it to me that my child be academically challenged?
- How important is it to me that my child's school be a nurturing and supportive place?
- How does my child do in large groups?
- Does my child need a lot of structure?
- How important is it to me to be connected to the school community?
- To what extent do I want to be involved in the daily life of my child's school?
- What kinds of sacrifices am I willing to make to have my child in a special language program?

for school language programs typically include foreign language immersion, bilingual programs, instruction in a foreign language, and academic support for minority language speakers in their home languages, as well as English as a Second Language instruction.

Choosing a School

Logistical Considerations

It is difficult to find a school that is a perfect fit for your child and family. Usually parents have to make decisions about what aspects of the school are most important. Making a list and trying to prioritize before researching and visiting schools can be helpful. It is also a good idea to think about your child's learning style and preferences. Practical considerations can make a huge difference in how well your child does at school. Parents may feel that it is selfish to consider issues such as drive time, childcare options or expense, but when these things are a bad fit, even the best program can turn out to be a bad experience for your child and your family.

The distance of the school from your home or work is an important consideration. How will your child travel to and from school? Will your child walk, take public transportation or a school bus, or will you have to drive? Is there carpooling, and how difficult would it be for you to contribute your share of the driving? Be aware that time pressure causes stress for everyone. If you are constantly running late for work, or your child is often late for school, mornings will be tense and unpleasant. Likewise, if it is a struggle for you to pick up your child from school or after school childcare, you and your child will be less relaxed and less able to enjoy your time together at the end of the day. For some busy families, time for sleep becomes an issue. If it takes more than thirty minutes or so to travel between your home and the school, you may be creating a situation in which your child will be continuously overtired. Parents should also think about how far children will have to travel to participate in extracurricular activities or to play with friends, and to what extent they themselves are willing to drive or otherwise arrange transportation.

Chapter Ten

In addition, parents must consider the impact of their school choice on the family's finances. Private schools tuition payments can be quite high, and any school might have expectations or requirements that families participate in school fund-raising efforts as well. At an expensive school where average family incomes are high, children may feel peer pressure to have high-priced clothes or other items. A language-oriented school may have opportunities for older children to travel, if families are able to afford the cost of the trip.

Parents who are interested in a private school, but are concerned about the cost, can ask about scholarships or tuition waivers. Some schools allow parents to contribute volunteer hours to fulfill fundraising or contribution requirements. Talking to other families in similar economic circumstances will give you a better sense of whether the school will be right for your family.

Parents should find out how the school encourages parents to be involved in their children's school experience. Children tend to do better at schools where there is significant parent involvement. Parents who are enrolling children in an immersion program teaching a language that the parents don't speak may be anxious about how they will be able to help their children with homework, or volunteer in the classroom. Many schools have special family nights. These may be social events or have an academic focus. In some schools there will often be a fund-raising component to such events. Parents should also make sure they are not going to take on too much responsibility at their child's school. A cooperative-style school may not work for a family has other time commitments.

Choosing a School

Parents will want to know the school's stated goals and values, and the community of the school. Some families want their children to go to school in the neighborhood. Families looking at language programs may already know families with children at a school because of their ties to that cultural community, and feel a sense of community there, even if the school is not close to where they live. Where your child goes to school will be a factor in who your child's friends will be. Peers can have a strong influence on children's perception of their family's minority language.

Visiting schools can be helpful in assessing whether a school feels right, and many schools offer tours or open houses for prospective parents. These can be useful because you are likely to have an opportunity to talk to teachers and administrators and ask questions. You will also see who else is interested in that school.

> "Teachers are so good here, very kind. In my own country, no one can ask anything to the teacher. The children get a slap on the hand, like this and I didn't like coming to the school, but my friend said in America parents have to go to meet the teacher and my son likes school."
>
> **—Denis,
> parent in Portland, Oregon**

It is a good idea to visit when school is in session, too. Many schools limit classroom visits by prospective families to minimize disruption for the students, but even if a classroom visit isn't possible, try to make a quick visit to the school during the regular school day, even if it is just to stop in at the office to pick up forms. You will have a better sense of whether the school is a friendly, welcoming place, whether the children and staff seem happy to be there, and whether children in the halls or playground are adequately supervised.

Chapter Ten

When you are talking to other parents about schools, remember that things at a school can change, sometimes fairly quickly. Also, your friend's children may be quite different from your children, so a school that was a good fit for them still might not work for you. Different parents will be looking for different things at a school. One parent is happy to see lots of artwork displayed in the halls, to hear a lively game in the gym, and a happy hum in the library. Another parent visiting the same school may notice trash in the hallway and two little girls running unsupervised on their way down the hall to the restroom.

It is important to talk to teachers or other school administrators about the school's philosophy and expectations, both for students and their families, especially if you went to school in another country. In the United States, parents are generally expected to make an effort to communicate about their child's progress with the school. Teachers may assume that parents who don't ask about their children, or participate in their children's schooling in other ways such as volunteering in the classroom, do not value education or are not concerned about their child's schooling.

Choosing a School

School Profile: Cahuenga Elementary School

Cahuenga Elementary School is an unexpected bright spot in the Los Angeles Unified School District (LAUSD). It enrolls over 1300 students, operating on a year-round schedule to alleviate overcrowding. About 85% of the students are learning English. Over 75% of them qualify for free or reduced price meals at school. Although class sizes in the early grades are not large (about 19 students on average), in fourth and fifth grades classes may contain 30 or more children. Student access to computers and other technology is limited. Its teachers have slightly less experience on average than teachers at other California schools. Yet parents have been known to line up as early as 2am on the morning of registration day to try to enroll their children at the school.

The children at Cahuenga Elementary are reaching higher achievement levels than at nearby schools. Students score higher on standardized tests. Comparisons of test scores of English language learners at Cahuenga with other schools in the district show Cahuenga students consistently score 10% higher than average on standardized tests of reading and math. The school has received a number of awards, including the California Association of Bilingual Education Seal of Excellence Award in 1998, and school staff members have qualified for merit bonuses for excellent performance.

What are the keys to Cahuenga's success? Observers point to the dedication of the principal, teachers and staff both to the children and to the notion that bilingual education works when implemented well. Given the high number of English language learners at the school, another important factor may be the relatively high percentage of teachers and staff who are actually bilingual. Opponents of Proposition 227, also known as the Unz initiative which was passed in California in 1998, pointed to Cahuenga as an example of how bilingual education could be a benefit, rather than a hindrance, to student achievement.

Even in the post-Unz era, Cahuenga is notable for its support of language education. The school offers special language support to Spanish-speaking English language learners, and a Korean/English dual language immersion program. There are students learning not only a second, but also a third language at the school. A child speaking Spanish at home may be enrolled in the Korean/English program, while another who entered school speaking only Tagalog acquires both English and Spanish.

Chapter Ten

Language programs are not the only positive aspect to Cahuenga for families in the neighborhood. The ethnicity of the teaching staff is also more reflective of the ethnic character of the school's student body than is typical at a California school. According to California Department of Education statistics, 46.4% of the teachers at Cahuenga are Asian-American, similar to the percentage of students who are of Asian descent, and 37.7% are Latino/Hispanic. Although the percentage of children who are Latino/Hispanic at Cahuenga is much higher, they are more likely to have teachers from a cultural and ethnic background similar to their own at Cahuenga, which can be a boost to children's self-esteem and motivation at school.

Also, although many of the teaching staff are relatively new to both the school and the teaching profession, Principal Lloyd Houske has been at the school for over fifteen years. In addition, most of the teachers at Cahuenga hold full teaching credentials in a school district that has been criticized for relying on too many teachers with waivers and emergency credentials. Parents are dedicated to the school, especially those who have children in the Korean/English dual immersion program, and this too may contribute to their children's motivation and academic achievement.

Because of severe overcrowding at the school, it is difficult to enroll a child at Cahuenga, even if one isn't after a coveted spot in the Korean/English dual immersion program. Estimates of how many children are bussed out of the neighborhood vary, but well over a thousand children line up each morning in front of the school. They board yellow school buses, riding for up to an hour to schools in different neighborhoods around the city. The commute lengthens the day for these children, making it more difficult for them to participate in extracurricular activities and complete homework. For those who qualify for a free breakfast at school, they may end up eating in class or arriving after lessons have already started. In 2002, a school bus driver strike further complicated the process of getting to school for these children.

"Ouch! My child has been rejected from preschool. It was a special public bilingual school with separate sections for the various languages. English had only eight places and they had 35 applications. From what I could glean from the letter, he qualified but it was only a question of places. We are talking about a three year old! I didn't go through this much grief picking a university!"

—Sharon, France

Choosing a School

The LAUSD has struggled with the task of constructing the new schools it needs. Plans for a new school to serve students in the Cahuenga neighborhood got off to a rocky start when district officials proposed building one large additional elementary school with a capacity of about 1200 students. The community countered with a proposal for 6 small schools of 400-600 students, but acknowledged that difficulties in obtaining appropriate sites and funding would require compromises. At present, a new elementary school with a capacity of 800 is in the planning stages, its award winning design resulting from the successful collaboration of the various groups involved in the planning process. However, even if the school operates on a year-round schedule, this new building will not be able to serve all of the children who want to attend school in their own neighborhood.

Public vs. Private Schools

The advantage of either a public or a private school depends on a number of factors, including the quality of both types of school in your area, the programs offered, and the degree of comfort you have with a particular school. According to a report by the National Center for Education Statistics, public schools in the United States tend to enroll a more diverse student population than private schools. Public schools also have more teachers and administrators from minority backgrounds. This may be a bonus to a family looking for a comfortable school for a child with a minority or mixed cultural and linguistic heritage.

Public schools in the United States also have to adhere to federal requirements to serve all students, even those with special needs. Families with limited financial resources who think their children may need extra language support should investigate the programs available through the public school system. Services available vary depending on the size and resources of the community, but may include English as a Second Language instruction, support in the classroom from bilingual aides, counseling for students having difficulty making cultural adjustments, and speech therapy.

Chapter Ten

One unfortunate consequence of the requirement to serve all students in a climate of limited financial support is that the resources of some public schools are stretched thin. Overall, class sizes tend to be larger in public schools than private schools. The degree to which this is true will depend on the specific area in which you live, due to the dependence of American public schools on local funding.

On the other hand, a public school will often be able to offer a greater variety of special courses, such as Advanced Placement or vocational classes, because it shares district-wide resources with other schools, because the school itself may be larger, and because of the public school mission to serve the needs of all children. Both public and private school teachers are more likely to send their own children to public school, although this fact could stem in part from the relatively low salaries of schoolteachers compared to other professionals. Public school teachers tend to be higher paid, have more advanced degrees, and stay in the profession longer, but private school teachers report being happier in their work.

Some parents have a political or philosophical commitment to public schooling. For others, a private school is simply too expensive. For parents who are able to choose between the two types of schooling, the best comparison will probably not be public vs. private, but a comparison between particular schools. The types of programs described here may be available in both public and private school settings.

Choosing a School

School Profile: Yew Chung International School

The Yew Chung Education Foundation operates several private schools internationally, all aimed at creating successful, bilingual graduates who can act as a bridge between cultures. The first Yew Chung School was established in 1932 in Hong Kong. There are now five campuses, including one in the United States, in California's Silicon Valley. The Silicon Valley school offers pre-school, kindergarten, and elementary school programs, all featuring two-way dual language immersion in English and Mandarin Chinese.

The Yew Chung educational philosophy is that it is possible to take the best ideas and practices from Eastern and Western academic traditions to create an engaging, challenging, and supportive learning environment. Yew Chung emphasizes academic excellence, a global perspective, and character formation in accordance with Christian principles. Yew Chung utilizes multiple intelligence theories of learning, and works to strike a conscious balance between encouraging independent thought and inquiry, and respect and concern for community. The goal is to produce eager life-long learners, who are bilingual, multicultural, and view themselves as international citizens.

Students are placed in one of three programs when they enter the school, based on their level of proficiency in Mandarin Chinese at entry. Students who start school speaking Mandarin as their first language are placed in the First Language program, where they immediately begin working on academic and literacy skills. In the Second Language program students with no previous experience with Chinese are encouraged to develop communicative abilities, and an appreciation of Chinese culture. The third track is a Pre-First Language program, designed for students speak some Chinese at home, but who are not yet fluent enough in Mandarin to start the First Language program. Students are expected to transition to the First Language program after one year.

School teachers and administrators do not guarantee a particular level of fluency in either English or Mandarin at any point in a child's school career, preferring to treat children as individuals who develop at their own pace. However, school graduates generally do very well academically. Yew Chung alumni have gone on to well-known institutions such as Cambridge, UCLA, and Cornell, and have been accepted at prestigious art schools, such as the Rhode Island School of Design and Chicago Institute of Art.

Chapter Ten

Yew Chung features small classes of about ten students, each with two teachers, one teaching in Mandarin and the other in English. The preschool program uses an integrated, theme-based curriculum to encourage children to develop creativity and problem-solving skills. There are both full and half-day options, and parents may enroll their pre-school children on two-day, three-day, or five-day schedules.

Elementary school teachers take a structured approach to teaching reading, writing, and math, while encouraging independent inquiry in social studies and art. Music appreciation, violin lessons, and physical education are also part of the curriculum. Extended day care is available at additional cost until 6pm. Summer programs offer opportunities to explore Chinese culture, as well as sports, arts, science, nature, and other theme-based topics.

Foreign Language Immersion

Some public and private schools offer foreign language immersion programs. In a public school system the program may be a magnet program to which families from all over the district may apply. The foreign language immersion program may be a special track within a school. Children who live in the neighborhood usually must apply to the special program along with children throughout the district, and may not be given any special consideration in applying. Especially popular programs often have lottery systems to determine who will be allowed to enroll, although it is common for both public and private schools to give preference to siblings.

Generally, no knowledge of the target language (the foreign language taught at the school) is required or assumed for kindergarten or first graders. Students wishing to enter at an older age may need to demonstrate some proficiency in the language. According to the Center for Advanced Research on Language Acquisition at the University of Minnesota, the majority of children in immersion programs enter at the kindergarten level with little or no previous experience with a second language.

Choosing a School

How a foreign language immersion curriculum is actually organized can vary. Some programs try to limit the use of the majority language to situations where a child is frustrated or upset, or to emergencies, in the first year or so. Other schools may use an approach providing children with foreign language immersion half of the time and majority language instruction during the other half. The advantage to this partial immersion system is that one teacher can teach two groups of children in the foreign language, an asset to schools in areas where qualified teachers with the necessary fluency in the target language are scarce. Partial immersion programs are popular with parents, too. Some parents are uneasy about their children being in a total immersion situation because they worry their children will suffer academically without any instruction in their native language.

Even schools that use the foreign language most of the time may include majority language instruction in a few targeted areas, such as literacy instruction. It is typical for a foreign language immersion program to set a goal for all children to be reading in both the school language and the majority language by the end of third grade, but some private schools may leave majority language literacy instruction completely up to the parents.

Foreign language immersion programs are usually associated with additive bilingualism, and children in such programs tend to do very well on standardized tests, although in some cases it takes a few years for their scores to catch up with peers in majority language schools due to the extra time needed to develop reading proficiency in both languages.

In partial immersion programs children are less likely to go through a period of lagging test scores in the majority language, but how well children will learn to speak the target language depends in part on how much time is actually spent using the language at school. Generally, children in partial immersion programs don't become as proficient in the foreign language as children in full immersion programs. If the language is used less than 50% of the time, the program might be more accurately described as foreign language instruction rather than immersion.

Chapter Ten

The linguistic background of the families enrolled can also have an impact on children's acquisition. If most of the children use the country's majority language together when not in the classroom, i.e. on the playground or when playing at each other's homes, children may think of the foreign language as a school-only language. Studies of foreign language immersion programs have shown that students do tend to use the school language mostly for academic work and the majority language for other kinds of interactions.

In a study of a small group of children in a Spanish immersion program, Dr. Maggie Broner of St. Olaf College in Minnesota found that the language children used at any given time depended on what they were doing, the content of the discussion, and the person with whom they spoke. Within the group observed for this study, one child who was more likely to use Spanish influenced children interacting with him to do the same. It may be that in programs where there are both children learning the language as a foreign language and children who speak it as a first language, the language may be used for a wider variety of purposes between the children.

"To dwell too much and too critically on the quality of French spoken by immersion students is a red herring because it ignores the fact that immersion students not only communicate effectively in French but also learn the skills of communication: selecting the right words with the right nuances, adapting communicative strategies to get the message across, cracking the right joke without making a cultural or linguistic gaffe, and establishing a positive environment with the native speaker."

**—Dr. Andre A. Obadia,
Canadians for French**

Choosing a School

School Profile: The German American School

This private elementary school in the Pacific Northwest began as a playgroup for toddlers, and now provides a German immersion program for students in pre-school through fifth grade. The school is housed in a traditional brick school building, leased from a public school district, incongruously overlooking a busy freeway exit. On the other hand, the location seems appropriate when one considers the school draws students from all over the metropolitan area. Students can continue with their German language education after elementary school by attending a nearby private middle school with several language tracks, including a new German program developed in collaboration with the German American School.

The school's approach incorporates Howard Gardner's theory of multiple intelligences, and uses an art and music infused curriculum based on seasonal and nature themes. The school tries to combine the best of German and American styles of education, with high expectations for student achievement in math and science, and a collaborative approach to learning. Classes are small, and the school also offers formal instruction in music and fine arts. Students may enter with no previous exposure to German through first grade.

Teachers strive for exclusive use of German in preschool and kindergarten, with English used only when a child becomes confused or frustrated. In first grade, English is used about 20 % of the time, and formal instruction in English language arts begins during the second half of this year.

Through a partnership with a nonprofit childcare provider, the school offers free before-school childcare, and after-school care is available on site for a fee. Saturday school style classes in German are held after school and are open both to students enrolled at the school and to those who attend school elsewhere. The school also has German language summer school programs for both its own students, and students enrolled at other schools.

Maintaining stable funding for the school is an issue the school administration is trying to address. Because the school has been in operation less than ten years, it does not have a substantial endowment or a large pool of alumni families to tap as potential contributors. The school solicits funding from corporate donors, and receives a small grant from the German government.

Chapter Ten

School Profile: "Somos Unos...We Are One"

The New Jersey Department of Education provides a variety of language education services to public schools in New Jersey through its World Languages Program. For example, Englewood Public School District in Englewood, New Jersey participates in two different programs, one offering foreign language instruction and the other a dual immersion magnet.

All students in Englewood Public Schools receive instruction in Spanish as a Foreign Language, meeting for 45 minutes with a Spanish teacher, 4 times a week. In 1997 Englewood also began a dual language English/Spanish immersion program that is housed by three different schools in the district. The magnet program is popular with both Spanish and English-speaking families, and is seen by the district as a cost-effective way to promote second language acquisition.

Demand for the Dual Language Program outstrips capacity, so a lottery system is used to determine who may enroll. Children beginning the program start at Quarles School for kindergarten and first grade. The program is expanding, and there are now four classes at both the kindergarten and first grade levels. For grades two to four, children move to Lincoln School, where there are six dual language classrooms. At Dismus Middle School there are currently two sixth grade dual language classrooms. It is expected that the magnet will continue to expand.

The program's goals are to develop bilingual, biliterate and bicognitive skills in English and Spanish, to maintain academic achievement, and to promote cross-cultural understanding and appreciation. The program uses a 50/50 model, with children spending half of their time at school in each language. Children in the program are predominantly Latino or African-American, reflecting the ethnic make-up of the district. Class sizes are kept small, with about 18 students in each class, even through the 6th grade. The biggest challenge the Dual Language Magnet has encountered thus far is in recruiting enough qualified teachers.

Choosing a School

Bilingual Education in the United States

A discussion of bilingual education could be a book onto itself, even if the discussion were limited to the United States. Bilingual education has been a contentious issue in the US for decades, as critics have questioned both the goals and the effectiveness of bilingual education methods, while advocates point to the potential cognitive and social benefits to children who speak a minority language. Bilingual education proponents blame the lack of adequate funding, a shortage of highly qualified bilingual teachers, and the high-risk student populations they often teach to explain the perceived failures in some schools. The controversy has led to the passage of a number of measures in American southwestern states abolishing bilingual education in public schools.

Although there are a variety of ways in which bilingual education programs are designed, usually students receive instruction in both their minority language and in the majority language upon school entry. The English language instruction typically includes English as a Second Language classes, as well as some content-based instruction in subjects like math and social studies. Children also receive instruction in academic subjects in their minority language, including literacy instruction. In traditional bilingual education, children who speak only their minority language would be placed in a separate classroom with other children with the same first language. Other methods, such as two-way immersion, group children speaking a minority language and those speaking the majority language together. In other cases, a group of children speaking a minority language might be placed in an English language classroom with the support of a bilingual teacher or aide.

Specific criticisms of bilingual education in the United States are that the method is slow to teach children to speak English, that it segregates language minority students, and it doesn't present students with sufficient academic challenge. Critics of bilingual education tend not to be educators, but rather prominent community members such as businessman Ron K. Unz, who championed the so-called Unz initiative in California. Many of these critics are

Chapter Ten

professionally or financially successful immigrants who strongly believe their acquisition of English was instrumental in their ability to achieve their success and they're concerned that children in bilingual education won't have an equal opportunity for success because they will not be pushed hard enough by the school system to learn English.

As a practical matter, children usually learn the majority language of the country they live in no matter what schooling they receive. Some children in the United States do struggle academically, and there are some, especially those who move frequently back and forth to their home country, who may not become proficient in English. However, most immigrant families to the United States have completely replaced their minority language with English by the third generation. The question of whether bilingual education is effective really concerns whether a system that supports a child's native language will delay acquisition of the majority language or whether, as bilingual education advocates claim, it gives the child stronger language and academic skills overall.

In fact, current research in education and language acquisition support the theory that bilingual education is most likely to promote academic success for language minority students. Benefits of bilingual education include increased motivation and self esteem, higher scores on standardized tests than children of similar socioeconomic background who speak only one language, better understanding of grammar and nuance, and the advantage students later enjoy as bilinguals in the job market. However, it is difficult for researchers to control for factors such as the variety of program methods and curriculum used in bilingual education, and it is also difficult to separate issues such as socioeconomic class and immigration from the debate, so many people remain unconvinced of bilingual education's advantages.

Many bilingual programs enroll only children who are native speakers of a minority language, and are designed to teach the majority language while helping children maintain their minority language skills. Generally, children are first expected to read in their minority language, with the assumption they will be able to transfer this skill to the majority language relatively quickly. They also receive academic instruction in both languages.

The goals of those who support and those who oppose bilingual education are different. For bilingual educators, it is important that students eventually speak, read, and write English well, but this is only one of the goals. In bilingual education, it is considered equally important that children develop age-appropriate oral and literacy skills in their minority language. One reason is those skills can then support English language and literacy development, leading to a more solid foundation of skills in English as well. It is also

Parents interested in the on-going debate on bilingual education in the United States can contact some of the following organizations for information from both sides of the issue:

- **The National Association for Bilingual Education (NABE)** is a non-profit organization promoting quality bilingual education for language minority students in the United States. Contact info: NABE, 1030 15th St., NW, Suite 470, Washington, DC 20005 www.nabe.org

- **The National Clearinghouse for English Language Acquisition & Language Instruction Educational Programs (NCELA)**, funded by the U.S. Department of Education, provides information on bilingual education. Contact info: NCELA, 2121 K Street NW, Suite 260, Washington, DC 20037 tel: (800) 321-6223 www.ncela.gwu.edu

- **English for the Children** is a California-based group, with significant Latino membership, which is concerned about what it describes as the failure of bilingual education to adequately teach students English. Contact info: English for the Children, 555 Bryant St., #371 Palo Alto, CA 94301 www.onenation.org

- **English First** is primarily a lobbying group with the goal of promoting English as the official language of the United States. Contact info: English First, 8001 Forbes Place, Suite 109, Springfield, VA 22151 www.englishfirst.org

Chapter Ten

believed children should acquire certain concepts and knowledge when intellectually ready, and if they are not at a level of proficiency in English that would allow them to explore those new ideas, they should be introduced in the students' minority language.

Generally speaking, bilingual education detractors believe the primary goal is to get children to an age-appropriate level of proficiency in English, and that if striving for bilingual language development delays that process it is not in the best interests of the child to continue in both languages. Some fear that bilingual education will actually hinder acquisition of English, in part because children will be less motivated to learn a new language in a bilingual school situation, especially if they live in communities where many people speak their minority language.

Children can become conversationally fluent without having the skills they need to cope with more complex language tasks. Children who seem to be doing well in elementary school may suffer academically later when the work expected of them at school becomes more demanding. In part as a result of some of the gaps of skills and knowledge that can occur when children go through a school system in a second language without native language support, there is a relatively new phenomenon in some universities and community colleges in the United States. Increasingly, colleges and universities are offering English language classes designed for residents who may be beyond traditional English as a Second Language classes, but still need support and instruction in how to do certain tasks, like professional or academic writing.

Choosing a School

School Profile: Rogers Middle School

At Rogers Middle School in Boston, which enrolls approximately 700 students, about 60 students in grades 6-8 whose first language is Vietnamese participate in a transitional bilingual Vietnamese/English program. The program's goals are to enable students to become proficient in English while maintaining their Vietnamese, and to give them the skills they need to succeed academically. The curriculum of the bilingual program is designed so that students in the program are as integrated as possible into the school. Students take some classes with mainstream students, and are sometimes formally paired with a buddy in those classes. Students in the bilingual program are highly motivated, as evidenced by the nearly perfect attendance rate. The program is also popular with parents, who enjoy meeting the Vietnamese teachers and aides from the school in the community.

English as a Second Language (ESL) Instruction

English as a Second Language programs in the schools are implemented in a variety of ways, depending on the needs and resources of the community. In public school settings, parents must give permission for their children to be placed in special education programs, including ESL. Placement can be appropriate for children in bilingual families, if they enter school speaking only the family's minority language. Parents will want to consider the amount of English language support their child may need, whether the type of program seems to be a good fit, and the age of their child. Children entering school in pre-school or kindergarten may have enough time to catch up with their peers in the majority language without special ESL instruction, especially if the family has other resources with which they can support the child's learning. Students in later grades may be at risk for falling behind academically, and are also more cognitively prepared to take advantage of direct instruction of grammar, vocabulary, and so on.

Chapter Ten

Children in ESL programs may be grouped together according to the minority language they speak, but in many communities there are not enough children who speak the same language to make this possible. Therefore, the ESL teacher may not speak the child's minority language. He or she will probably be trained in teaching English as a Second Language, but there are some districts that do not require a special endorsement for ESL teachers. Even in districts where there is no specific ESL endorsement, however, an ESL teacher may have years of experience in teaching English as a Second Language, and special endorsements in literacy instruction. Teachers may even have a separate degree in teaching English as a Second Language, in addition to their teaching credential.

Parents in bilingual families are sometimes concerned that if their children are placed in ESL programs, they will be segregated from mainstream students. Pull-out models of ESL instruction address this issue by placing students in regular classrooms for most of the day, with students attending English language class with children who have similar needs. Students may be drawn from different classrooms within the same school, or from different schools. Districts which don't have enough students at a school to support a full-time ESL teacher must decide whether the teacher will travel or the students will.

Choosing a School

Contained ESL programs are either 'early exit' or 'late exit' programs. Early exit programs are designed to move children into mainstream classrooms as early as possible, and may have a time limit of a year or so for participation. Children are often assessed primarily on the basis of their oral proficiency to determine whether they are ready to move out of ESL. The curriculum may include some content instruction, but is mostly intensive English language. Early exit program are appealing politically, and to some families, because they focus on quick results. Critics say that early exit programs may place children in regular classrooms before they are ready, where they become overwhelmed and struggle academically.

Late exit programs incorporate instruction of academic subjects into their curriculum, and assume that it will take children some time to develop literacy skills in English, even after they have a certain level of oral proficiency in the language. Teachers use a structured approach and comprehensible language to teach students in subjects like math, social studies, or science. The curriculum parallels the mainstream classrooms, with the idea that students won't fall behind in other subjects while developing their English skills. Late exit programs often have bilingual teachers and try to group students who speak the same minority language together. Detractors of late exit programs believe when students speaking the same language are together with a bilingual teacher they don't have enough motivation to learn English. Another problem opponents of such programs point to is that when speakers of different languages are together, and there are no teachers or aides who speak the children's first language(s), children are likely to be getting overly-simplified content in the other academic subjects.

Chapter Ten

School Profile: The International Community School

The International Community School is an alternative high school program in Oregon established through the joint efforts of two non-denominational Christian charitable organizations and the local public school district. The school provides educational services primarily to immigrant and refugee high school students, from the former Soviet Union, Mexico, Central America, Southeast Asia, Africa and the South Pacific, who are struggling in regular public high schools because of cultural and linguistic differences. About 15% of the students are not newcomers to the United States, but have difficulty in school because of cultural differences.

There are 73 students currently enrolled, with small class sizes and individual tutoring available. Bilingual teachers and staff are able to provide students with translation and support. Their curriculum focuses on literacy instruction, along with English as a Second Language. Students are placed in an English language class based on their proficiency. As their English improves, students begin taking regular high school course work for credit. Classes in a range of subjects are offered, including literacy in students' native languages and electives in classes like filmmaking, speech, and creative writing. Some students eventually move to a mainstream school to finish high school.

A number of students are placed in the International Community School because of difficulties in cultural adjustment as opposed to linguistic difficulties. Students who are the first in their families to attend high school work toward graduation with all the extra support the school is able to provide.

Choosing a School

School Profile: Newcomer High School

Newcomer High School in San Francisco was one of the first newcomer programs in the United States, and has served as a model for other programs nation-wide. Newcomer programs are designed to meet the needs of students who have newly arrived in the United States. Students are coping with a variety of challenges, including the need to learn English quickly, and negotiate a new educational system, as well as make cultural adjustments. Students at Newcomer High School are predominantly Asian (about 60% in 2002) and Latino (35% in 2002), with over 22 countries of origin currently represented within the student body.

The San Francisco Unified School District has twice proposed closing or moving the Newcomer program in recent years, once in 1998 and again in 2000. Some district administrators say they worry that the students at Newcomer High School are too isolated, putting them at a disadvantage when they try to make the transition to regular high school. Other district concerns are that some students stay at Newcomer beyond the recommended one year, and that the school is too small to offer many advanced academic courses. On the other hand, Newcomer supporters point out that for students whose most pressing need is English proficiency, earning credits in advanced courses may not be a realistic goal.

Newcomer Principal Herb Chan notes that the separate program and location have many advantages for students who have just arrived in the United States. The school is prepared to support students enrolling at any point during the school year. Because the school is relatively small, with only 326 students enrolled in 2002, it is able to provide nurturing environment. Students also appreciate being with classmates who are going through the same process of cultural transition.

Chapter Ten

The school provides three periods a day of intensive ESL instruction, compared to the two periods a day of English language support offered ESL students at other high schools. Students speaking either of the school's two major languages, Chinese and Spanish, also receive instruction in core academic subjects in their native languages. Other students receive the same course work in sheltered English instruction, a method of teaching academic content in English while accommodating student's limited English proficiency. Students are able to earn credit toward graduation while at Newcomer.

Support staff at Newcomer HS help to provide students and their families with connections to social service agencies, if needed. The school also partners with the organization YouthCares Partners in Learning program to provide peer tutoring and support after school. Most Partners in Learning tutors are immigrants themselves, teenagers who have successfully negotiated the process of cultural transition to life in the United States. Newcomer students also participate in programs such as WritersCorp, which brings writers in to schools to work with at risk youth, and the Education Enrichment Program of the San Francisco International Diplomacy Council, which brings speakers to talk with high school students in the Bay Area on a variety of international issues.

Newcomer has strong community support, especially from the Asian-American community. When the school district was considering relocating the program in 2000, many students, staff, and community supporters attended meetings to demonstrate support for their school, emphasizing the uniquely supportive and welcoming atmosphere and the special needs of its students. Business leaders and the local Asian newspaper also advocated on the school's behalf.

Choosing a School

Two-Way/Dual Language Immersion

Two-way immersion programs, also known as dual language immersion, are a relatively new way to teach children with two languages. They are popular both with families who speak a minority language at home and those who speak the country's majority language, but want their children to be bilingual.

In the United States two-way immersion programs are typically in public schools. Most two-way immersion programs are currently found in California, Texas, and New York, but there are programs in other states as well. Often two-way immersion programs are special programs within a particular school, rather than school-wide programs. Like foreign language immersion programs, there is a high demand and schools may use a lottery system to determine who is accepted. In the US, most two-way immersion programs are Spanish/English programs, although there are also programs in Chinese/English, French/English, Korean/English, and Navajo/English.

In two-way immersion programs, children who speak one or the other of the programs' target languages as native speakers are enrolled in roughly equal numbers. Instruction is given in both languages, with the goal of promoting bilingual language development for both groups of children.

Two-way immersion has a number of advantages over traditional bilingual education for language minority students. Because there are native speakers of the majority language in equal numbers, the children who speak the minority language are not segregated. Seeing other children learning their language, and that the school community values it enough to teach it, raises the prestige of the language in children's eyes.

For children who speak a majority language, two-way immersion programs are an appealing way for families to promote bilingualism. Children will have classmates who speak the target language as a first language, increasing their motivation to learn so that they can communicate. They also have the chance to experience the culture(s) of the language firsthand. Because at least some part of the school day is conducted in the majority language, parents tend to be less concerned their children will suffer academically by starting school in a foreign language.

Chapter Ten

Two-way immersion programs are implemented in different ways in terms of how much time is spent using each language. Some programs take a 50/50 approach, using both languages for an equal amount of time. Others use a 90/10 model. In this approach, instruction begins in kindergarten with the minority language being used 90% of the time. Each year the amount of instruction in the majority language increases, so that by middle school children have instruction in each language about half the time.

Teachers in two-way immersion programs may or may not be bilingual, but usually teach in one language, with two teachers sharing a classroom by teaching at different times during the day, or on alternate days.

Programs take different approaches to teaching children to read and write. In some cases, children are separated into native language groups when they first begin reading, and instruction begins in the native language for both groups. Other programs begin instruction in reading and writing to all children in both languages simultaneously. Still others start with reading and writing instruction for all students in the minority language, adding majority language literacy instruction to the curriculum later.

Elizabeth Howard and Michael Loeb, who interviewed teachers in two-way immersion programs for a study with the Center for Applied Linguistics, found that teachers overall felt positively about this type of program. Teachers mentioned that parents who spoke the minority language felt they were more valued in the school community, which increased the likelihood they would volunteer or otherwise become involved. Teachers also believed that children who started school speaking the minority language were learning English more quickly in two-way immersion programs than in other kinds of programs.

Choosing a School

Some teachers felt that the majority language of the country was still overemphasized in some subtle ways. For instance, English is often the language used to conduct staff meetings. One newly minted teacher, in describing his experience student teaching in a two-way immersion program, noted there were ways in which English dominated despite the best intentions of the school staff. He pointed out that the English-speaking families were more likely to have a parent who volunteered in the classroom, and these parents often did not speak Spanish. Due to the funding situation at the school, parent volunteers were a valuable resource, but in this case, their presence tended to increase the amount of English being used in the classroom.

School Profile: St. Procopius Elementary School

St. Procopius Elementary School is located in the Pilsen neighborhood of Chicago's inner southwest side. The school offers a dual Spanish/English language program for students, who are mostly Mexican-American. Some students are recent immigrants to the United States, while others are third or fourth generation, entering school speaking little or no Spanish. Tuition is low, about $1200 a year, and many families receive scholarships. The school is small, enrolling approximately 250 students in Pre-k through eighth grade. The Pre-k program is accredited by the National Association for the Education of Young Children (NAEYC). The school was recently named one of 20 notable Catholic schools in the Chicago area by the Chicago Archdiocese because of its language and cultural programs. The dual language program at the school is a relatively recent development, and one that did not occur without some difficulties.

Irish and German immigrants first settled the neighborhood where St. Procopius Church now stands, later moving on and making room for immigrant Czechs and Poles. The Czech community built St. Procopius Church, and the neighborhood takes its name from the city of Pilsen in Bohemia. In the late 1800s, St. Procopius School taught bilingually, in Czech and English. Over the next century, the population in the neighborhood gradually shifted again, as families of Czech descent moved to more suburban areas, and newcomers from Mexico began arriving in the 1960s. Participation in the parish community dwindled, and the church struggled with how to adapt its mission to the needs of the current community. By the early 1990s, the parish elementary school was suffering from financial problems, low enrollment and a lack of parent involvement. Many of the Mexican-American families who attended St. Procopius Church did not send their children to the school.

Chapter Ten

In 1991 the Catholic Archdiocese of Chicago asked Chicago Province Jesuits to staff the parish, and see what could be done to address the needs of what was now predominantly a Mexican-American community, with a substantial number of newly arrived immigrants. As part of the Jesuit plan to better serve the parish, the church began hold a Spanish language mass, traditional Mexican holidays were observed, and efforts made to provide educational and social services needed in the neighborhood. Dual language programs were planned for both the elementary and high school levels.

Katherine Beeman was principal at St. Procopius Elementary from 1995 to 2002. She hired the school's first Spanish-speaking teacher in 1995. The transition to a dual language program began slowly, with Spanish first being used as the instructional language for art class in grades one to four. Resistance came from all fronts, including teachers and many families attending the school. At one noisy meeting in 1995, some parents expressed anger at the decision to teach Spanish at school.

"The Jesuits had presented their plan to the school community," explains Ms. Beeman, "and announced that we were moving into the area of dual language instruction. We had some very angry parents who are Hispanic but who do speak English. These parents got up in the meeting, yelling 'This is America! How dare you take time out of the school day to do Spanish! We will do Spanish at home.' At this point, the Jesuit priests and I asked all those families that were not in favor of the program to leave. We explained that there were very many, fine Catholic schools right in the neighborhood that were not dual language, but that followed the instructional model that St. Procopius had once been. We helped those families find other schools."

In the art class, children initially struggled with Spanish. Even those who spoke Spanish at home discovered they did not have appropriate skills for using the language at school. There were some discipline problems as a result of the students' frustration. Other teachers were not supportive of the project. At the end of 1995, eight of the 10 teachers at the school decided to leave.

Choosing a School

Because the dual language plan initially called for adding Spanish language instruction only in pre-k and kindergarten in 1996, and adding a grade each year thereafter, those teachers would have continued to teach in English. However, they were uncomfortable with the direction in which the school was moving, and unwilling to make other changes, such as committing to stay after regular school hours to work on curriculum development and provide extracurricular activities for the students. On the surface, the teachers' departure was a setback for the school, but it provided an opportunity to implement radical change more quickly. Ms. Beeman decided to start school-wide Spanish as a Second Language through science, in addition to beginning dual language immersion in the early grades, hiring nine new teachers.

The school year began in 1996 with more students enrolled than had been during the previous year, due to an intensive recruitment effort of neighborhood families interested in dual language education. The school now plays an important role in a newly vibrant parish community, and benefits from many business and community partnerships. There is a new playground, an on–site school nurse, after-school activities and homework help. The Dual Language program continues under the direction of new principal Thomas Denneen, who previously served as assistant principal at the school.

Dr. Liliana Barro Zecker, a professor at DePaul University's School of Education who was involved in research at St. Procopius, describes the school's strengths as she saw them during her visits.

"St. Procopius," Dr. Zecker observes, "had a successful bilingual education program because of strong leadership in the principal, community involvement, committed, well-prepared teachers, and well-planned curriculum. The delivery of the curriculum was also theory-informed. The principal knew a lot about bilingual education, valued it as an educational asset for all students, and understood the school's mission as one that had to deliver the best possible educational opportunity for the students (to grow bilingual for a global society). At St Procopius, bilingualism was not considered a deficit to be fixed, but rather an asset, a goal to be achieved."

A public school teacher who sends her own child to St. Procopius explains her decision to 'go private' by pointing to the language opportunities that her child would not have if she attended the public school in her neighborhood. Her daughter entered school speaking only Spanish, she says, and the Mexican Legal Defense Fund has recently filed suit against her family's home public school district, citing a lack of appropriate academic support for Spanish-speaking students. She likes the fact that St. Procopius strives to present a positive image of Mexican-American culture. The curriculum at St. Procopius is challenging. Most importantly, she says, at St. Procopius her daughter is happy.

Chapter Ten

School Profile: Atkinson Elementary

Approaching Atkinson School, a public school in Portland, Oregon, from the busy street outside, one is immediately struck by the huge banners hanging on the front of the building. Designed to catch the eye of drivers and transit riders, they feature greetings and welcomes, and sometimes information on registration or upcoming events, in five different languages. Once inside the school building, the visitor hears a hum of activity from the multipurpose cafe-torium, serving as lunchroom, gym and auditorium space. Children's artwork decorates the hallway, with captions on pictures in English, Spanish, and Chinese. Notices to parents on the PTA board are in Spanish, Chinese, Vietnamese, and Russian, as well as English, and in response to a recent school satisfaction survey, 96% of the children and 97% of the school's parents agreed with the statement their school was a good one.

Atkinson prides itself on diversity. In 2002-2003 just under half of the 536 students enrolled were of European-American descent. Most of the other students are either Asian-American or Latino, and with some African-American and Native American children enrolled. Despite the fact that nearly half of its students start school speaking a first language other than English, approximately three-quarters of the children are meeting state mandated achievement levels by fifth grade. The school works hard at increasing parent involvement, offering evening ESL classes for the community, and parent computer nights in different languages.

All students at the school learn a second language. Families can apply from all over the district to a two-way Spanish-English immersion magnet program. A two-way literacy program in Mandarin Chinese is also available. The school provides English as a Second Language support to students who require it, as well as reading and writing instruction in native languages for children who speak Cantonese, Spanish, Russian and Vietnamese. The school also participates in one of two district-wide distance learning foreign language programs that provides instruction in Spanish for two hours each week. Additional classes in Spanish and Mandarin Chinese are available after regular school hours.

Acquiring enough funding to continue its programs is a continuing worry for Atkinson staff and administrators. The state and district in which the school is located is currently undergoing a significant funding crisis, which may result in a shortened school year and significant staffing cuts. Because of the population it serves and the efforts of its staff, the school has obtained grant money to help supplement the funding it receives from public sources. However, funding is a constant concern.

Choosing a School

Non-Immersion Foreign or Second Language Instruction at School

Until recently, it was common for school children in the United States not to have the opportunity to start a second language until high school. As research evidence accumulates and makes a stronger case for the need to start languages earlier, school systems have responded by offering second and foreign language instruction in the younger grades. How successful are these efforts? Can parents assume their children will learn a second language at school? Are these classes appropriate for children who also speak the language at home?

When children spend just half an hour or so a day at school studying a new language, most will not become fluent speakers, even after years of study. Even with the best teacher, the experience is not intensive enough. The language experience for children also tends to be artificial, so they don't necessarily make connections with the language in other parts of their lives. Rather than using the language as a medium for other learning or to participate in other activities, as language is meant to be used, the language itself is the subject. Children may not have any chance to use the language outside of the daily lesson, either at school or outside in the community.

It can be a challenge for schools to provide quality instruction in a second or foreign language to everyone who wants it. There may not be enough teachers available. In addition, foreign language is still viewed as enrichment, rather than an essential part of a core curriculum, so it tends to be one of the first subjects to be cut, along with things like art and music, when school funding is tight.

Whether or not children have opportunities to use the language outside of school makes a significant difference in their language acquisition. Immersion experiences such as summer camps, vacation trips, or short-term exchange programs for older children are usually beneficial for children learning a foreign language at school, although children are sometimes discouraged to find they're not able to use the language as well as expected.

Chapter Ten

Students who've learned a language at home sometimes participate in foreign language classes in the language at school, with mixed results. There are children who will pretend they know less of the language than they do, so as not to appear too different from the other children. Parents may find their children are developing an accent, so they sound more like their classmates, or even the teacher, if the teacher is not a native speaker. Some bilingual children are sometimes bored, yet others enjoy the opportunity to excel and share their knowledge with the class.

Students who speak a language at home may enroll in foreign language classes, especially in high school, as a way of getting an easy credit. It can be embarrassing for some students to discover their grammar or writing skills in the language are relatively poor, but the class can provide them with an excellent opportunity to improve. Some high school students find such classes to be a good way to expand their knowledge and abilities in their minority language. When advanced level classes are available, bilingual children can take advantage of the chance to explore the literature of the language, or to receive advanced instruction in grammar. It is common for students to have language arts instruction in the majority language at school, and there is little reason for students who want to have it in their minority language as well not to do so, if the instruction is available.

16

Choosing a School

16 S   **Profile: The Moshi Hola Project**

ne Moshi Hola Project is an experiment in distance language learning for ele-
school children. Students in kindergarten through fifth grade in the Portland
chools in Portland, Oregon tune in five days a week to watch interactive program-
esigned to teach Japanese (**Moshi Moshi**) or Spanish (**Hola Hola**). Schools pay
to subscribe to the program, with access to extra materials and training for class-
teachers on how to use the programs. Schools outside the district may also join.

he idea is that by accessing the program, even teachers without knowledge of a
ond language are able to introduce one to their students. Classrooms that use the
ogram most successfully are those that use the Moshi Hola Project as a basis for a lan-
,uage curriculum, but bring in other supplementary language resources. In some classrooms, parents who speak Spanish or Japanese help out, reading aloud in the language or
bringing in culturally related projects for the children to do. Volunteering in **Moshi
Moshi** classrooms has also become popular with Japanese college exchange students in
the city.

Children are given short vocabulary quizzes periodically, but assessment of student
learning is otherwise up to the teacher. The program is also available on cable, so families can record the programs and use them for home viewing. There are also homeschool-
ers who participate in the program.

Parent, teacher, and student satisfaction with the programs depend both on expectations and on the effort made to supplement the programs with other opportunities to
learn the language.

As one teacher put it, "With Hola Hola you don't get much beyond 'hola! hola!' but as
an introduction it's very nice."

Others are more enthusiastic. The Moshi Moshi project has been running longer and
has some especially ardent supporters. Parents say their children talk about their Moshi
Moshi lessons, and enjoy going on line at home to use the activities and games available
on the Moshi Moshi web site.

Chapter Ten

School Profile: The Dwight School

The Dwight School is a selective, private school located on Manhattan's Upper West Side, at 89th Street and Central Park West. It was founded in 1872, and boasts an illustrious list of alumni. Graduates include Henry Morgenthau, Secretary of the Treasury during Franklin D. Roosevelt's Presidency; Fiorello LaGuardia, Mayor of New York City; master builder Robert Moses; theatrical producer Hal Prince; artist Roy Lichtenstein; and writer Truman Capote. High school graduates are often headed for the Ivy League, or schools abroad such as Oxford or Cambridge. The school motto is that each child has a spark of genius, and its goal is to produce compassionate, thoughtful global leaders. For those who can afford it, The Dwight School provides an outstanding education.

The Dwight School emphasizes international citizenship and cross-cultural communication. Students begin language study with French in kindergarten. In sixth grade, students may add Spanish or Latin to their studies. High school students have a variety of language study opportunities, including Dutch, French, Spanish, Latin, German, Italian, Japanese, Hebrew, Chinese, and Arabic. Language acquisition is facilitated by study abroad experiences, for example to Costa Rica, Normandy, and Prague. Students are encouraged to take advantage of study abroad opportunities from the fifth grade onward.

English as a Second Language (ESL) support is available, either individually or in small groups, depending on the current needs of English learners within the student body. Newly admitted students may enroll in summer ESL immersion programs in order to gain a head start on their English language acquisition. Older students may receive coaching for the TOEFL test, required by most U.S. colleges and universities from foreign students seeking admission.

School curriculum includes peace education and philosophical inquiry, and is based on the International Baccalaureate (IB) program. The IB diploma program is an increasingly popular curriculum for high schools around the world wanting to offer their student body an academically rigorous education with an international focus. The Dwight School is unusual in the United States in that it offers the IB program at three levels, beginning in kindergarten.

Choosing a School

The Dwight School strives to offer its students a well-rounded education, and has the resources to do so. The school is ideally located for field trips to visual arts galleries, and for visits from working artists. Professionals also come in to do workshops with drama students, and there is an annual trip to London with a theater focus. Music students participate in an annual recital held at Carnegie Hall. Athletic opportunities include swimming, tennis, basketball, soccer, yoga, judo, and fencing. The school has produced a number of nationally ranked fencers. The school offers a special short-term academic support program designed for students who are struggling, especially those who may be affected by a learning disability.

Admission to the Dwight School is competitive. The admission process includes a by-reservation open house for parents, applications, separate interviews for parents and children, and standardized test scores. Most students enter at kindergarten, sixth grade, and ninth grade. Kindergartners are tested through the Independent Schools Admissions Association of Greater New York, in cooperation with the Education Records Bureau. Families may submit recommendations, if they choose, and children who have attended other schools, including pre-school, are expected to produce transcripts or school records.

Chapter Ten

Saturday Schools

Saturday schools provide formal instruction for children learning a minority language at home and can be a terrific opportunity for children to make connections with the world in ways parents alone can't facilitate. Children can make friends with other kids like themselves, who speak the same language at home but also live, like they do, within the majority language and culture.

Saturday schools can equally be a tremendous source of tension in the family. Children sometimes resent going, and parents find themselves irritated with the complaints, even angry or hurt that their child is not more enthusiastic about the opportunity. It helps if the style of the program is a good fit for your child, and if they know other children who attend.

The term Saturday school refers to the fact that classes are most often held Saturday morning, but such classes may be held at any time. The degree of formality and the curriculum vary widely, so parents should make sure they understand what the program is like before enrolling their child.

In some countries, such as Sweden or Australia, Saturday programs are government funded and operated. In the United States, administration of such programs tends to be local and funding comes from a variety of sources, including parent tuition.

A Saturday school program could be an informal arrangement initiated by parents. With younger children it may be more of a playgroup. Parent volunteers may serve as teachers in some Saturday schools. Larger and more established programs generally hire teachers, although the program coordination and administration may continue to be done by volunteer parents. Saturday schools are also sometimes organized by expatriates living abroad temporarily for work to ensure that their children won't be too far behind in school when they return home.

Choosing a School

Some Saturday school programs consist of classes offered through cooperation with foreign language departments at universities or community colleges. Classes sometimes take place on campus and may be taught by university professors or instructors of the language, or by teachers hired just for the Saturday school program. Teachers in such programs may be experienced language teachers, but can have varying degrees of experience working with children.

Governments of the home countries may contribute sponsorship money, usually a relatively small amount, to language schools, including Saturday schools. Such sponsorship may require certain things are included in the school curriculum, usually conforming to the national curriculum standards for schools in the home country. Other Saturday school programs are sponsored by religious institutions and may include religious instruction.

The fact that a program is being held in a church doesn't always mean that the school is church-sponsored. Churches often make their space available to non-profit groups as a service to the community. Saturday schools may be an extension of programs offered by private schools, such as parochial schools, in certain ethnic communities. There are a few Catholic schools in the Chicago area, for instance, that offer classes on Saturdays in Polish language and culture.

Parents should find out what the goals of the school are, whom the school is intended to serve, and what sort of a curriculum the teacher uses. For example, the South Carolina Japanese Language Supplementary School states the school is intended for Japanese children living abroad who will at some point be returning to Japan, although other children whose needs would be served by the school may be allowed to attend. The German American School Association, which operates a number of Saturday schools throughout Southern California, aims to serve any family with an interest in having their child learn German.

Chapter Ten

Most Saturday school programs assume that families are using the language at home at least some of the time and the school program is a complement and supplement to the language exposure children are receiving at home. Parents who want to introduce their child to a second language they themselves don't speak would be better served by classes and schools prepared to teach the language to non-native speakers. Some Chinese language schools in the United States make an effort to accommodate the needs of families who have adopted children from China who wish to enroll their children.

Li Zhang, a parent volunteer at the Springleaf Chinese School in Portland, Oregon explains, "Most our children are come from families who speak Mandarin. However, we have quite a few children where only one of the parents speaks Mandarin. And we do have several children, who are Chinese, adopted by American families who do not speak Chinese at all."

"Based on my experience, I think bilingualism is easier under the following conditions. The child learns from his/her peers in a playful, fun environment. Most kids are force-fed by parents and in schools; too authoritarian! Enjoyable cartoons and movies are great learning tools. My daughter could recite every line in Japanese of an entire animated movie! Use it or lose it. Unless people use it frequently, language gets rusty fast. It takes me days to get back into gear in French and Spanish. Language learning is viewed like stamp collecting, a key to foreign cultures, but there needs to be a practical purpose for learning it."

—Sherida Tatsuno, Aptos, California

Choosing a School

Classes designed for children who will be returning to school in the language's home country may put more emphasis on curriculum that children might not be getting at school during the regular week which would put them at a disadvantage when they return to the home country. Subjects might include the literature or history of the home country. They could include special subjects not normally taught in the schools of the country where you live. For instance, Japanese schools in the United States often emphasize advanced math skills, due to the relatively high level of math achievement expected in the Japanese school system compared to the United States.

Other Saturday school programs, designed for children of immigrants, place an emphasis on language and cultural learning. At the Springleaf Chinese School, art is taught along with Mandarin Chinese. Some schools directed at immigrants may focus on literacy, especially for languages that use a different writing system. For example, the Farsi School of Seattle holds classes for six- to nine-year-olds for one and a half hours each Saturday afternoon, primarily in reading and writing in Farsi. Saturday schools sometimes work to prepare high school age students to take Advanced Placement exams, enabling them to receive foreign language college credit.

Saturday schools may have homework, which some families find helpful in maintaining consistent academic contact with the family's minority language throughout the week. Other families may feel that homework in addition to that assigned by the child's regular school is burdensome.

Some Saturday schools are rather old-fashioned in their teaching methods. When parent volunteers are teaching classes, lessons may be based on their own school experiences, which can be outmoded. Children may be expected to sit quietly at work, and there can be a lot of rote memorization or worksheet activities. Since Saturday school often begins to interfere with other extracurricular activities, such as sports or music, it is a good idea to find a Saturday school program your child actually enjoys.

Chapter Ten

As with any school, it is helpful to talk to other families who have children enrolled to find out what aspects of the school they and their children are happy with, and if they have experienced any problems. Before enrolling your child, you should determine whether the school and school's expectations fit your family's expectations.

Aside from the language contact and opportunity to learn about culture(s) related to their minority language, children often enjoy the chance to make friends who have a similar heritage and background as themselves. However, when parents insist that their children give up other opportunities, such as playing sports, or participating in other extracurricular or social activities in order to attend extra school, children's resentment can spill over to the language itself.

Choosing a School

School Profile: D.A.N.K. German Language Schools

D.A.N.K. stands for Deutsch Amerikanischer National Kongress, or German-American National Congress. It is an organization dedicated to promoting cultural exchange between Germany and America. There are about 30 chapters of D.A.N.K. in the United States. Nine of these chapters run language schools for children and adults as part of their mission to promote friendship between the United States and Germany, and a positive image of German-Americans.

A structured approach is used to teach German language and culture. Children are placed in class by language proficiency, and age groups are mixed. Families are encouraged to visit classes before enrolling to ensure that the program will fit their needs. Classes for children are held after school or on Saturdays, with additional classes for adults in the evenings.

The Chicago North School is the longest established of the D.A.N.K. schools. Chicago North has a waiting list for the pre-school program. The school also runs a tots program for children nine months to three years with games, stories, and songs. Parents attend with their toddlers.

Families belonging to D.A.N.K. also have access to a monthly bilingual newsletter, and may participate in cultural events, such as dances or festivals. D.A.N.K Chicago North shows German language movies on Saturday afternoons. The Fox Valley school, also in the Chicago area, offers movie rentals, and video conversion so that families can send playable tapes to relatives in Germany. Many of the D.A.N.K. schools are located in or near Chicago, but there are also schools in Pennsylvania, and a relatively new school in Phoenix, Arizona.

Chapter Ten

School Profile: Emilia Plater Polish School

The Emilia Plater Polish School is a large and lively Saturday school in Schaumberg, Illinois. Over 600 students from pre-school to high school age attend the school. There are 23 School Board members, who play an active role in school operations. Classes are from 8:30 to 12:30 on Saturdays at a local high school. There is a final exam at the end of the year, and the school also holds graduation ceremonies. Throughout the year the school holds special events, such as spelling bees, poetry recitals, and other performances by the children.

Parents are expected to assist with supervision at recess, and to otherwise participate in the life of the school. Each school year Emilia Plater usually has at least one or two fundraising dinners, with raffles and live entertainment. In addition to supporting the Polish language program, these serve as community building events, giving parents a chance to socialize with other Polish families whose children attend the school. The school also organizes celebrations of important Polish holidays, and celebrates more typically American holidays, such as Halloween. Santa Claus and the Easter Bunny pay visits, and distribute chocolate and other goodies. On Polish Constitution Day on May 3rd the school marches in the city's annual Constitution Day parade.

NORWAY, SWEDEN,
FINLAND, & DENMARK

FINLAND

SWEDEN

NORWAY

Trondheim

Vaasa

Bergen
Oslo

Turku Helsinki

Stockholm

Göteborg

DENMARK Alborg

København   Malmö

Chapter Eleven

18 ## Literacy in Two Languages

Spoken language is merely a series of squeaks.
— **Alfred North Whitehead**

Is it Necessary for Bilinguals to Read in Two Languages?

Just as most bilinguals are not equally fluent in speaking both languages, most do not read both languages with equal ease. In fact, many bilinguals only read in one of their languages. Helping bilingual children learn to read and write in both languages will require an extra commitment of time from families, and possibly of money, too, because of the necessity to provide materials. Many families find the process goes better when children are formally instructed, whether by a tutor, in school, or in a Saturday school. Parents are not always their children's best teachers.

159

Chapter Eleven

Celia, looking over Laura's extensive collection of comic books in Portuguese, "Can you read all these?"

Laura, aged seven replies: "Not really, I left Brazil when I was four."

When the two languages have completely different writing systems, learning the rules and symbols for both does take some time. Although learning to *speak* two languages simultaneously from birth is often a successful strategy for bilingual families to follow, it is more common for those who read in more than one language to learn to do so sequentially, rather than at the same time. Ideally, children learn to read first in their strongest language. When the written forms of the child's two languages use the same script, children may transfer their reading skills from one language to the other with relative ease.

Even as adults, bilinguals who read in both languages often read more slowly in one language than the other. This may be because the reading strategies they've developed learning to read one language don't work as efficiently when reading the other. Parents who want their children to read and write in both languages shouldn't worry if those skills are much stronger in one language than the other, as long as the child is performing well enough to keep up at school. For children to be biliterate is a significant achievement even if skills are not equal in the two languages and children will be able to build on early reading skills later in life.

One difficulty arising when children read much less fluently in one language than the other is they may favor the stronger language in their selection of reading material, or even avoid the weaker one altogether. This can affect their subsequent learning, so the weaker language becomes weaker still.

Whether or not parents decide that biliteracy is an appropriate goal for their children will depend on the role literacy in each language plays in the life of the family, and the resources at the family's disposal. Even if the family has not yet decided about reading in both languages, if children are being exposed to two languages from birth, it makes sense in terms of general language development to involve them with books, songs and stories in both languages.

Literacy in Two Languages

Some reasons for making the extra effort to help children read include the obvious potential advantage in employment later on, especially if the family's minority language is one that is spoken by a substantial number of people, or happens to be of special interest internationally, or in the country where you live. In the United States, the ability to read as well as speak Pacific Rim languages, and languages of the Middle East and Eastern Europe, is currently useful to job seekers, as is reading proficiency in global or regional languages like Arabic, Chinese, French, German, or Spanish. In the area where I live, it is common for employers in the fields of education, health care, and social services to require bilingual English/Spanish skills, including literacy in both languages.

Languages can also help open up academic opportunities, enabling people to study abroad or access information available in limited languages. Children whose parents have retained citizenship and close ties with the home country may be able to do some or all of their university studies there, if they have the necessary language skills.

Other reasons for learning to read in both languages are less obvious. The ability to read a language can be a kind of gateway to new information and experience. For example, learning to read in the minority language allows children to access a greater variety of information about the home country and culture, and to communicate with distant relatives in writing. Being able to use computer software or read for pleasure can also increase children's general motivation to use the language.

Children who are able to read their minority language can use that skill to make discoveries about the world and create connections in the language that go beyond their experience within the family circle. The possibility of using the language independently of the parent(s) providing spoken language input can help children find their own interests in the language, and to continue to use it as they move out into the world as teenagers. Some people later in life find themselves in situations where there are limited opportunities to speak one of their languages, but because they are able to read, they are able to maintain the less used language to a greater degree than they might otherwise.

Chapter Eleven

Motivating Kids to Read in Their Weaker Language: Ideas from Parents

Parents I asked admitted that this was an uphill battle, especially as children grew older. When the family's minority language was English, children seemed to be somewhat more motivated to work on their literacy skills, and got quite a bit of practice on-line. A couple of parents in the United States who had children enrolled in foreign language immersion programs admitted that when reading for fun the children preferred English.

"We're planning a trip, and letting the girls each choose a destination or something that we'll do. The catch is that all the information we're getting for planning the trip is in Italian. They complained, but I think they got the value of it."

—Gina Berkman

"I leave attractive books around, really nice big coffee table books with lots of photos. They do like looking at them."

—Maya

"My friend gives me her [Vietnamese] newspaper at church, and after [church] I cook and he reads to me."

—Ncog Dinh

"Germans have a lot of nice books and software and things for children. When it is something really attractive, she'll make the effort to use the German."

—Jessi Koeffler

"We've been encouraging our son to think about doing an exchange, and reminding him that school would be easier if he kept up on his reading in the language."

—David

Literacy in Two Languages

Learning to Read

According to Dr. Ellen Bialystok, a psychologist specializing in language development at York University in Ontario, being bilingual can actually help children learn to read because their bilingual language skills give them a greater awareness of the symbolic properties of language. Bilingual children already understand the name of a thing is not the thing itself, having learned that objects have different names in different languages, and this gives them a head start in the realization that written language represents the spoken word.

The term "emergent literacy" refers to the kinds of information about written language children have, and the kinds of experiences children have with books and other forms of written language, before they learn to read. All of these emergent literacy experiences contribute to the process of learning to read, whether children will eventually read one language or two.

One of the indicators pre-reading children are learning the kind of background information they will need to read later is pretend play that involves literacy. If your four- or five-year-old is making a "library" out of cardboard boxes, you probably don't have too much to worry about. Other types of play are when children look at books on their own while telling themselves the story, bring you their "grocery list" or "checkbook," or scribble you a "letter" with crayons.

Pretend play itself can indicate that a child is developing some of the cognitive abilities he will need to read because it demonstrates that he is able to think symbolically. When a child says, "Let's pretend the bed is an island and there are crocodiles on the floor," and his friend says, "No, it's a tree house," they demonstrate that they've moved far beyond the literal to the concept that one thing can represent something it is not.

Children who don't read yet, but are beginning to understand some things about written language often have some misconceptions about how print works. It is common for pre-reading children to assume that a word will have some of the properties of the thing the word represents. Just as a bed might work as an island or tree house in a child's game because of its size and shape, but not be acceptable as a flower or a cooking pot, young children might think that the appearance of a word should relate to the thing it represents. Children may think that bigger words, those made up of more letters or characters, are the words for bigger things, for instance.

Chapter Eleven

Teaching Reading:
Whole Language vs. Phonics

When parents think about teaching their children how to read, flashcards, cassettes, or CD-ROM sets often come to mind. Many of these are based on a system of teaching reading popularly known as phonics. On the other hand, much of the advice parents receive about supporting children's reading skills involves shaping the environment, so that children's interaction with written language occurs naturally, i.e. reading to your child every day, visiting the library often, making sure they have crayons, paper, and a place where they can use them. This kind of advice has its roots in a whole language philosophy of teaching reading.

There used to be energetic debates in education over the relative merits of the Whole Language and Phonics approaches to teaching reading. Parents of bilingual children, who are trying to teach their children to read at home, at least in one of their two languages, often worry about whether they are choosing the right method, without understanding completely what these two approaches are.

Todd, an elementary school teacher, says of the difference between the two methods of teaching reading, "We've created a false dichotomy in this country."

Kris, another teacher, agrees, "It's been said that when whole language came over the pond, phonics fell off the boat."

Whole language is an approach that emphasizes communication, purpose and meaning in written language. Essentially, whole language means that reading should take place in a context that is meaningful to children. Rather than emphasizing phonemic awareness, teachers encouraged children to learn "sight words" they would recognize as a whole, and to construct the meaning of new words through contextual clues.

In American schools in the 1970s and '80s, whole language was a popular idea, but was sometimes interpreted to mean that focusing on sound-symbol relationships was problematic. Some felt phonics was an inauthentic way to teach reading because it reduced an act of communication to a mechanical process of code-breaking. However, some basic decoding skills are obviously necessary to gather the meaning from written language, and many children don't learn how to do this

Literacy in Two Languages

on their own. For some children, remembering "sight" words may not come easily. They may not have much opportunity for straight-forward practice and memorization if their teacher is not much in favor of flashcard drills, which in more extreme interpretations of whole language would be meaningless.

At the other end of the spectrum, phonics-based methods of teaching reading emphasize decoding sound-symbol relationships, which are then put together to form words. Some believe that children who learn to read with this system become more accurate spellers. (In languages like English, however, because a letter or letter combination may have a number of different corresponding sounds, a certain amount of sight word memorization is often a component of good spelling.) A completely phonics-based approach may involve practicing with drills to the point of boredom for some children. On its own, a phonics-based approach tends to not to be very motivating, although some children may enjoy the repetition of drills more than an adult might think. Some children learn to "sound out" words, but unfortunately have little comprehension of the meaning of the text they are reading. Progressing beyond this stage can be difficult if a child has been turned off by the drills and exercises, and now dislikes "reading."

Current methods of teaching reading tend to incorporate a blend of techniques from whole language and phonics-based approaches. Parents who want to try a systematic approach to teaching reading at home should probably fo' v this approach as well. They should also consider how their child seems t   rn. A strong auditory learner may do well and enjoy learning to read thr   gies that help build phonemic awareness. Visual learners may quic'   og-nize sight words and sequences, and benefit from whole lang   ie language the child is learning to read is an important co some writing systems may require memorization of sig'

Beginning to Read: Thinking and Learning About Prin*   n-
by Dr. Marilyn Jager, MIT Press, 1990 is a ge   ..ar that
parents who are concerned about the   arn   very
acy development. Dr. Jager does i   ..it a great deal
skills, but it is a good primer on th   ..ng and practice.
to read, especially for parents who
English as one of their two languag .

Chapter Eleven

Knowledge and Skills Transfer Across Languages

Learning to read is not just a matter of learning to decode the symbols on the page, although that is the part of the process of which we are generally most aware. Before children can begin to read in the decoding sense, they have to know many things about written texts. First, they need to know why we read things, and why we write things down. They need to understand the relationship between spoken and written language. They need to know that the marks on the page mean something. Ideally, they are intrigued and start trying to figure out how they can get involved. Children have to see a purpose in literacy in order for the process of learning to read to begin.

There is other information children must have before they can begin to decode what is on a page, or write their own messages. They need to know that written words represent spoken language. For most written languages, they learn there is a system of sound-symbol correspondence that enables people to know how the word they are reading should sound. They also learn the form of written language differs according to the function of a text. In other words, a storybook will look different from the television schedule, which in turn looks different from a street sign.

Fortunately, this is all knowledge that applies to any written language. When learning to read in two languages, a child doesn't have to learn everything about the process twice. Many concepts will transfer. Even if a child has learned in English, for instance, the words run left to right, and the opposite is true in his or her other language, the child still is aware there is a standard way of doing these things, that words are not just sprinkled randomly across the page.

Some strategies transfer across languages, too. For example, good readers in all languages generally employ the strategy of making reasonable guesses. What this means is that even if your family uses the minority language at home exclusively, the literacy-related experiences your child has in that language provide support for learning to read at school, even if that instruction takes place in the majority language.

Literacy in Two Languages

On the other hand, not everything a child learns in one language will transfer to the other, and the experiences children have in each language with literacy will have an impact on their abilities to use literacy skills in certain ways in each language. For example, a study conducted by a researcher at Harvard University, which examined French/English children's ability to tell a story in each language while looking at a wordless picture book, found that children's experiences with picture books in each language affected their performance in telling the stories in the same language. All of the children were attending school in French, and had similar exposure to storybooks in French while at school. Their exposure to English storybooks differed depending on their home environment, although the children were all rated at a similar level of oral proficiency in English. The children who had been read to in English were able to tell more detailed and coherent stories in English than those who had only been read to in French. The implication is that children do not necessarily transfer literacy skills, such as storytelling conventions, learned in one language to another.

Learning to Write

Before children are able to write, they need a certain level of fine motor skill development. They need to be able to hold a crayon or pencil, and to control the marks they make on the page. Coloring, drawing, and toys that require some manual manipulation all provide this kind of practice.

At first, children "write" by making squiggles and scribbles on the page, often incorporating drawings as well. What is important is that children at this stage have figured out that it is possible to represent meaning on paper. Soon, children are using some identifiable letters. They may assume the parent will understand the message they meant to convey, even though they won't be able to read it back to themselves. Children use symbols, pictures, and letters in combination to try to express their meaning.

As they refine their understanding of the process of writing as communication, children start writing in different genres. One piece of writing is a "letter," while another is a "book." As children get older, depending on their

Chapter Eleven

experiences, they may distinguish between books that are stories, and those that are non-fiction, relating information they know about a certain topic. Children may produce their own calendars, lists, newspapers, or other types of writing they have encountered, and usually begin to understand that spelling and punctuation can affect how well they are able to communicate their message. This motivates them to work on accuracy.

Children learn to write because they have a reason to write, generally a message they want to communicate to someone. Being overly critical about spelling can be discouraging to the fledging writer. Many good readers are not good spellers; the two skills don't seem to be necessarily correlated. In reviewing your child's written work, asking questions about spelling, punctuation or handwriting form that prevents you from making sense of the message will probably be enough to encourage your child to improve. When your child reaches an age that seems appropriate, providing him or her with a dictionary and instruction on how to use it is useful, too.

When Should Children Learn to Read in Each Language?

Debates over the efficiency of bilingual education aside, it has become quite clear in the language research and education community that children learn to read more easily when they also learn to read a language they speak well. Therefore, one of the issues arising when parents try to figure out how to help their children develop biliteracy skills is how to time reading instruction in each language. Most children aren't ready to read until school age, and then they'll be instructed in reading in the language of the school, likely to be the majority language. What happens when they are stronger in the minority language when they begin school?

Current research in education indicates that children learn to read faster and achieve higher levels of literacy in general if they begin with their first language. Bilingual families who have chosen to speak only the minority language at home and plan to have their children learn the majority language at school should consider working on literacy in the minority language at home. This doesn't mean formal instruction, necessarily.

Literacy in Two Languages

Although it may work for some families to bring out flashcards, work on character recognition, and so on at home, some children will be turned off by this kind of thing, especially if they are not really ready for it. A more diffuse approach may work better for many families, with parents reading aloud, providing children with access to books and other forms of written material, paper and crayons, letter blocks or magnetic letters, encouraging word games, and modeling literacy skills themselves. For parents who do want to take a more formal approach to learning to read at home, helping children to learn "sight words" beginning with the child's name and other favorite words often works well as a starting point.

When the language of the school is the majority language, children who don't speak that language well face an extra challenge of learning to read a language that is less familiar to them. It takes more time and may be a stressful experience, which can affect their attitude towards school in the long-term. On the other hand, there are children for whom this situation is a challenge, but not one that has long-term negative affects. The extent to which this is harmful depends on how much academic support they are receiving in general, and in their minority language in particular. Small class sizes, the presence of bilingual teachers or aides in the classroom, or even a literacy-rich language environment at home in the child's other language can help to make learning to read a more positive experience.

It is important to communicate with your child's teachers, to convey your interest and high expectations for your child, and to ensure they understand your child is working on two languages, so you can coordinate your efforts. Most schools have conference times scheduled each year, but teachers expect to meet with parents at other times, too, and generally appreciate parental interest in what their child is doing at school. If you feel you need the support because you're not fluent in the language of the school, ask a friend or relative to come with you.

Chapter Eleven

How Parents Can Support Literacy Development in Two Languages

Keep in mind that developing literacy skills takes a long time, and children begin that process when they are very young. Whether or not children successfully read at school, even when taught first in their weaker language, depends on their general literacy experiences, regardless of the language. A child who sees everyone reading around him, who is encouraged to talk about storybooks, to look at comics or the weather report in the newspaper, who visits the library, and has access to paper, pencils and crayons, will likely be motivated to learn to read and write when he gets to school, even if those experiences are mostly in the family's minority language.

In one language or two, the best way to foster your child's literacy is to provide an environment rich in language and print, and to make sure they have positive experiences relating to texts and the printed word. The effect of the family environment on children's later experiences with literacy has been researched extensively, and it is clear that these early years are very important. Ironically, the earliest is likely to take place without the parent really being aware of it. Your child observes literacy in action from the back seat of the car watching you read maps and street signs to drive to a play date. When you call your mother, write down a recipe she gives you over the phone and cook with it, you demonstrate the value of literacy again.

Some researchers believe the way that we talk with our children also has an impact on their later literacy. Lively dinner conversation has been associated with later literacy achievement, as has encouraging children to talk about their day or interesting events, asking open questions, encouraging them to make predictions or explain their thought processes in coming to a conclusion. These ways of talking relate to later levels of literacy skill in part because they reflect ways that we use written material. It may also be that these kinds of conversation support strong verbal skills and this gives children an advantage in learning to read.

Literacy in Two Languages

Word and letter games come more naturally to some parents than others, but these can be a good way to support your child's early learning. Playing rhyming games can help children recognize that words can be broken down in smaller parts, and that the word is changed when a sound changes. Identifying shapes helps with character or letter recognition. Parents can encourage children to look for the shape of a character or letter in their name in pictures or designs, or in the environment while out for a walk or a drive. Other kinds of traditional driving games can be useful, too, such as looking for all the letters in the alphabet on signs while driving, or looking for out-of-state car license plates.

With children who are beginning to read on their own, you can encourage them to make good guesses about what an unfamiliar word is, or what it might mean, by asking them to look for clues. These clues could be information from the rest of the sentence or the story, pictures, or even information they already know about the topic or the kind of story they are reading.

Storytime

Most parents read to their children for a variety of reasons. They understand it is important for their child's language and later literacy development, but they also read aloud to their children because they enjoy it. Children enjoy storytime, too and it is part of the child/parent bonding process to sit on a parent's lap, cuddle, and to have the parent's attention.

Talking about pictures in a book helps even the youngest children begin to understand there is a connection between spoken language and what is on the page. As you are reading, you can point to pictures of things familiar to your child, and talk about them. Maybe the cat in the book looks like your cat, for instance. Let children initiate some discussion, and ask questions about what they think might happen next, but don't get so busy asking questions that you both lose track of the story.

Chapter Eleven

Don't expect babies or very young children to spend much time listening to you read. While there are toddlers who can sit for fifteen minutes or more looking at a book, most will be ready for something else in a few minutes. Looking at books should be enjoyable for both of you, and won't be if you are trying to keep a squirming toddler on your lap and paying attention because you haven't finished the story. Choose books that are sturdy, and recognize they will not stay in pristine condition. Toddlers have been known to teeth on books. That can upset parents, especially when they are books in the family's minority language and hard to find.

Look for books that rhyme, or have predictable elements. Most children love the familiarity of recurring phrases, which is one reason why stories such as *The Three Little Pigs* are perennially popular. Stories that have repeated phrases are easier for children to remember, enabling them to pretend to read while looking at the book on their own. This kind of pretending gives a child confidence, in addition to being fun.

Create a special place for your child's books and magazines. Some families like to have separate locations for books in each of the child's two languages.

Reading aloud can be more complicated if each parent speaks a different native language. In many families one parent tends to read aloud more often, so the child tends to get more exposure to being read to in one language than the other. When a parent is a fluent speaker, but not a native speaker of the language he or she uses with the children, reading aloud may not be as enjoyable for that parent. Because people often do read more slowly in a second language, some bilingual adults find they are not able to read as fluently, easily, or with as much expression in their non-native language. Children themselves often notice the difference and may express a preference for parents reading in their native languages.

Finding appropriate books in the family's minority language can sometimes be a challenge. Although it is relatively easy to find books in some languages in the United States, Spanish or French, for instance, simple availability is not the only issue. Stocking the bookshelf can get expensive when it is necessary to shop at specialty stores or ship from overseas.

Literacy in Two Languages

Parents in the United States may have success looking for books and other media at the local public library, if their minority language is spoken by a significant number of people in the area. You may need to ask about materials available in other languages, rather than just searching the shelves. Books in certain languages may be located primarily in one branch location, usually where there are more library users who use those languages. Many library systems with multiple branches will send books over to your branch if requested. Some systems allow patrons to place holds, or reservations for items that are popular.

When the selection of books in a family's minority language is limited, other issues can be a problem for parents trying to interest their children in minority language books. Sometimes it is hard for parents to find books that are interesting and at an appropriate intellectual level for children in their weaker language. Parents may find that their children don't relate to books and other materials from the home country of their family minority language. Children may complain about books from cultures less concerned with producing entertaining children's literature, and may not have the depth of cultural knowledge required to make sense of some of the literature, especially books for older readers. Sometimes parents themselves find that books and other materials for children reflect cultural values they had chosen to leave behind.

Even children who love to read may not want to read in the family's minority language when they feel the selection is limited. When presented with shelves of books in one language and a small stack in the other, the lure of greater variety usually wins out.

Older children may enjoy reading translations of popular books, like the Harry Potter series. Some families find that incentives, financial or otherwise, work to motivate older readers. Some children find computer software or magazines on a topic of interest to them more motivating than books.

Although it is time-consuming, making books of family stories is one way to supplement your selection of books in the family's minority language. Depending on your skills, you can draw illustrations or use family photos to tell stories about your childhood experiences, relatives, or even the family pet. Most children enjoy stories about themselves, and this is a good use for all those snapshots most families have. Pictures from old magazines are another source of homemade picture book material.

Chapter Eleven

When our daughter was younger, we tried translating some books from English to Farsi ourselves because she liked to have what she thought of as real books in Farsi, and our selection was fairly limited. The added complication of the book needing to go from left to right in English and right to left in Farsi meant we had to rebind the books, so, not surprisingly, we didn't do very many of these.

Different Kinds of Literacy

The more ways a child experiences literacy, the more successful he or she is likely to be in developing literacy skills. When planning a strategy for helping your child to become biliterate, as well as bilingual, it's worth thinking about whether literacy in each language serves different functions in your household, what those functions are, and even how you might expand on those opportunities for literacy experiences for your child. The way children think about literacy, in general, but also in each language, will depend on their surroundings.

Pre-school children may use their emerging awareness of literacy to make cards or books, menus or lottery tickets, depending on their experiences. When children grow older, they begin to see some of the more subtle nuances or uses of literacy, such as when we may choose to write to someone rather than speak face-to-face, or that there are certain kinds of transactions that involve writing. As they become more knowledgeable about written language, bilingual children will begin to notice when and for what tasks family members use each of the family's languages in the written form.

Literacy in Two Languages

Parents are sometimes unaware of the real extent to which the majority language has permeated their home, especially in the form of written language. It may be that when speaking everyone uses the family's minority language, but what language are they reading? Take a look around your home. What kinds of books, magazines and other printed materials do you have in your family's minority language and in the majority language of your community? When members of your household write notes or messages to each other, what language do they use? Look at your walls. If you have posters or decorative items hanging, is there any writing on them? In what language? Open the cupboards and look at the product labels on the things inside. What language are they in? Take a look at the pile of mail on the counter, and the notes attached to the front of the refrigerator. What language(s) do you see?

Parents who are biliterate may assume the value of biliteracy skills will be obvious to their children, but it is important to look at what your child will observe in his or her daily life. Use the following checklist to see what uses for literacy your child is likely to see for each language at home.

Chapter Eleven

During a typical week, which of the following activities would your child see you or someone else in your household or another household member doing, and in what language?

1. Reading books

In your family's minority language____

In the majority language ____

2. Reading a newspaper ____

In your family's minority language____

In the majority language ____

3. Reading a magazine

In your family's minority language____

In the majority language ____

4. Reading work-related material

In your family's minority language____

In the majority language ____

5. Reading mail

In your family's minority language____

In the majority language ____

6. Writing letters

In your family's minority language____

In the majority language ____

Literacy in Two Languages

7. Making lists

In your family's minority language____

In the majority language ____

8. Studying

In your family's minority language____

In the majority language ____

9. Using a computer

In your family's minority language____

In the majority language ____

10. Writing messages for other household members.

In your family's minority language____

In the majority language ____

It is not uncommon for bilingual families to have quite a few children's books in their minority language, but little other written materials in that language. Predictably, as children get older and begin using their literacy skills for purposes beyond reading children's books, such as using a cookbook, writing a message, checking the TV schedule, or reading the comics in the newspaper, they use the language everyone else in the house is using to accomplish those tasks.

Chapter Eleven

Ten Tips for Raising a Strong Reader
(in One Language or Two)

Adapted from materials provided by the American Library Association

1. **Talk and sing** to your baby.

2. **Use board books** for babies, and make "reading time" cuddle time.

3. **Make regular trips to the library,** and help your child see it as a fun place by taking advantage of special programs that take place there, like story-times, puppet shows or other performances.

4. **When he or she is old enough**, let your child get his or her own library card.

5. **Give books as gifts**; this reinforces the idea that books are special and fun.

6. **Use recorded stories** and books in the car, or during quiet times. Many libraries have recorded books available for check-out, or you can record yourself reading some of your child's favorite stories.

7. **Take advantage of waiting time** at the doctor, dentist, or while at another child's activity. Bring along favorite books or magazines.

8. **Enroll school-aged children** in summer reading programs available at many libraries.

9. **Ask your older child to read aloud** to younger siblings, or to you, or to the dog. Self-conscious readers may prefer to read to the dog.

10. **Make sure your child** sees you reading, too!

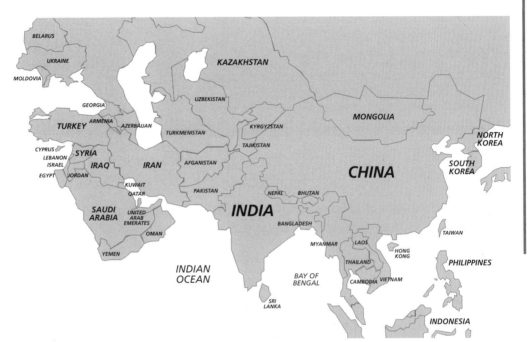

Chapter Twelve

Biculturalism

"I met a young girl in San Diego the other day at a convention of mixed race children, in which the common habit is to define one parent over the other. In most white and black marriages, the habit is to define black over white. But this girl said that her mother was Mexican and her father was African. I said, `What are you?' She said, `Black-xican.' And I think to myself, `You know, the vocabulary that the Spanish empire has, the recognition of multiplicity of possibilities, we do not have words to describe who we are anymore. And if we rely on the old vocabulary, we are doomed because no one is using it anymore. They're inventing their own words. Yes."

—Richard Rodriguez

Chapter Twelve

The term bicultural seems to imply a division, a line down the middle, two things within a whole, two cultures, separate and distinct, existing within one person. In reality, just as bilingualism is not usually balanced, biculturalism isn't either. Children with an interest in their cultural heritage (and math) sometimes enjoy calculating the fractions of each culture or nationality that make up their background, but few people behave in ways that indicate they are exactly half of one thing and half another.

> **Anna, living in the United States,** had beautiful leather shoes for school that her mother had ordered from Europe. Every morning Anna cried when she had to put them on, and begged her mother to be allowed to wear tennis shoes to school, like the other children.

People often feel most rooted in one culture, although they are aware that the other has influenced their lifestyle, values, and so on. There may be certain areas of their life that reflect one culture, while in other areas they draw more on the other.

A bilingual, bicultural adult living in the United States might work in an American corporation and behave according to the norms of American culture while at work, but come home to a lifestyle more reflective of their minority language's culture. That person's co-workers might not even be aware of the extent of his or her biculturalism, and be surprised upon visiting the home. Other times the bicultural person may carry more of their minority culture with them to work than they realize. Bicultural adults might slip into one cultural style when interacting with parents, and the other with a spouse. How one interacts with friends might depend on the cultural context in which the friendship was formed.

For children it can be much the same. They may have a home culture and an outside culture, although the home culture is undoubtedly going to be affected by their experiences in the majority culture. The culture at home may be more of a blend, especially if the parents are each from different countries.

> "My son will be American, but I want him to be a little bit Mexican, too."
>
> **—Bernarda Aguilar, USA**

Biculturalism

How children's friends react to their biculturalism will affect how they feel about it. Even if it isn't possible to have a social circle of others with the same mix of cultures, seeking out situations where there are other multicultural families will help children to feel this is a normal way to be. Books, movies, dolls, and toys reflecting diversity can help, too, and are worth seeking out.

There are also the so-called third culture kids, children of diplomats, international businesspeople, or those who work in international organizations. These children have a home culture, that of their parents, and the culture of the country in which they live, and then a third culture, a kind of blend of cultures, which they may share with other children like them.

Parents who are themselves comfortable with their culture and their place in the mainstream society around them are better able to help their children be comfortable with their multicultural upbringing, and proud of their cultural heritage.

Acquisition of Culture

Like language, culture is not something children will acquire unless they have a great deal of exposure to it. This is something that both parents and children may not realize. People often assume language is culture, and language does tend to reflect a certain cultural point of view. It isn't exactly the same thing, however.

When visiting relatives from the minority language culture, children may be disappointed when they don't feel comfortable or understand what is going on, even when they know the language. Parents can be embarrassed their children are behaving inappropriately without recognizing the children are unaware of what it is they are doing wrong. Seemingly small things, like an inappropriate gesture or way of making eye contact, can make a bad impression, even if the relatives know the children don't know exactly how to behave because they've been living elsewhere.

Chapter Twelve

Families who learn a second language which the parents don't speak as native speakers, either by using it at home or by going to a foreign language immersion program, should realize it is possible to learn to use a language without feeling a sense of cultural identification. When children learn language at school, they may restrict its use to school settings and even to academic tasks at the school, using the majority language to chat with friends at lunch and recess. Although it is possible for children to have a certain level of knowledge about the culture of the language they're learning, through literature and art, social studies and participating in school celebrations of holidays, this is not the same thing as feeling as though they are Japanese, or French, or German.

It is also possible to have a strong sense of cultural identity that involves belonging to a certain ethnic group without speaking the language. It is not uncommon for certain groups in the United States to retain a strong ethnic and/or cultural identity, even when many members of that group don't speak the language. Parents who are motivated to raise bilingual children primarily because of cultural identity may discover it isn't actually necessary for them to speak the language in order to participate in community life. This, of course, can make motivating them to acquire the language more difficult.

Deciding on Biculturalism

Like the decision to raise children with two languages, the decision to raise children with more than one culture is sometimes driven by necessity, other times more by choice. In cases where one or both parents are immigrants, it is in the interest of family harmony to make some conscious choices about culture, as well as language, because the culture of the minority language will probably have some impact on the children's lives, whether parents intend it or not.

Children often behave, especially in more visible and superficial ways, according to the norms of the majority culture, which can be quite irritating to parents at times. There may even be occasions when children identify strongly with the majority culture on more significant issues, such as the acceptability of living together before marriage. Sometimes children worry about their cultural identity because although they feel more akin to the majority culture, they're also concerned that not identifying strongly with the minority culture is an act of betrayal toward their parents.

Some decisions about the family's cultural choices will be easier to make at the outset of starting a family, like whether or not to live in an area where there are other families from the same ethnic group, or choosing certain holidays from the minority culture to celebrate as part of the family's traditions. Other decisions will come up unexpectedly along the way.

Although a bicultural couple will probably realize they're going to have different ideas about dating rules for the children, and make a point of discussing these things, it can be a surprise to find they also have different ideas on when it is no

Chapter Twelve

longer appropriate for little girls to run around without a shirt in hot weather. In addition, it can take awhile to figure out what value differences are at the root of arguments over the number of after school activities that are appropriate for children, or how important it is that they take that advanced calculus class during senior year of high school. Recognizing the underlying value is usually an important part of the process of making cultural decisions in bicultural families, because sometimes it is not possible to do a little of each, or to do something halfway between what each culture would dictate. Understanding the values involved helps parents to come up with creative solutions everyone can live with.

When each parent is from a different culture, one culture or the other usually dominates the culture of the home. If the family is living in a country where one parent was raised, that country's culture tends to be dominant. It is important to ensure that the culture of the minority language isn't denigrated, and this can be more difficult than it sounds. There may be stereotyping of the minority culture within the majority culture where the family lives and this can even occur within the extended family.

People outside the family may assume that when a family is having problems, this is related to cultural difference. Parents too may assume their bicultural children who are having behavioral or emotional difficulties are reacting to dealing with two cultures. In fact, every family has its problems and many children go through stages of difficult behavioral or emotional problems, even if they are not bicultural.

Examples of Cultural Differences

In families with parents from two different cultural traditions, there can be disagreements in areas that directly affect children, such as how children should be raised, gender roles, and how to relate to members of the extended family. There are obvious differences that come up in bicultural families concerning things like food and holidays, but it is probably the more subtle effects of culture that can cause more problems. When children see their parents finding solutions that are respectful of both cultures, those occasions when conflicts arise due to differences in culture can be learning opportunities for the children.

Even when the cultural difference is clear, figuring out what to do about it may not be. Regarding something such as food, for instance, although it would be nice to decide the family's meals will be from one culture half of the time and half of the time from the other, in reality it may depend on who does the cooking most often. It is sometimes difficult to find all the ingredients or cooking implements needed for one culture's cooking. One culture's style of cooking may also be more labor intensive and time consuming, which may not fit into the lifestyle of the country where the family lives.

Examples of the more subtle issues that commonly arise in bicultural family life include how a person deals with time, the degree of sensitivity to body language, and how "cleaning the house" is defined. Even when the minority language parent is fairly assimilated in the majority culture, the family probably encounters other relatives or friends who act in ways more reflective of the minority culture, and this can create tension, too.

For some people, religion is an important part of their culture. Religious differences can be difficult to accommodate depending on the intensity the parents' practices and the philosophical distance between the two different religions. This is another case when satisfying both sides of the extended family can become complicated.

Chapter Twelve

Choosing the Majority Culture

Sometimes families consciously choose not to try to create the culture of their minority language in the home. In families in which one parent is an immigrant, that person may feel the responsibility of representing a whole culture for the children. This can be a very lonely feeling. When someone leaves their home country at a relatively early age, they may not have all the knowledge they need to recreate certain aspects of their home culture for children. That person may also be completely assimilated, and not feel a compelling need to pass on the culture of their home country. Parents may also not feel comfortable being bicultural themselves, and therefore want their children to have the security of being firmly rooted within the culture of the country where they live. Even when this is the family's choice, there are going to be ways that the minority culture affects family life. Sometimes these end up being attributed to idiosyncrasies of the parent's personality, rather than being recognized as being due to cultural influences.

Holiday Celebrations

One problem with trying to celebrate the special days and times of year of the minority culture is that these celebrations are often occasions for getting family and friends together. When you are far away from that side of the family, the holiday can actually be a sad time of missing home, family and friends. It can be hard to work up enthusiasm for celebrating in the traditional ways. Work schedules can also interfere with properly observing a holiday, and it may be difficult to find the right props and decorations.

On the other hand, as far as most children are concerned, the more holidays the better, so they are usually excited about holiday celebrations. Sometimes a scaled-down version of the traditional holiday works out the best. A celebration that goes on for a week or more in the home country might take place on a day or a weekend. This approach also has the advantage of allowing the minority language parent to choose the foods, rituals, and so on which are his or her favorites, and skipping the rest.

Biculturalism

In our family, my husband's memories of holiday celebrations tend to be from the perspective of a child, or teenager. It took a few years before we had any kind of rhythm to our preparations for the Iranian New Year because he was trying to remember exactly what, for instance, should be included in the Haft Seen, a special table with seven items starting with the letter S, and also to get used to being in charge of making the arrangements himself. We have still not figured out what to do with the living wheat grass traditionally thrown into water. He remembers it was thrown into a nearby creek during childhood celebrations. We live in the city with no creek near our house, and the two industrial rivers just don't have the same association with nature and renewal.

Visits to the Minority Culture's Home Country

The best way for children to become competent in the culture of their minority language's home country is to spend some time there. Parents often don't realize the limits of their children's knowledge about the home country and its culture, and so may not adequately prepare their children for the first trip.

Helen moved to San Francisco from Hong Kong with her family at an early age. Although she was indistinguishable from a native speaker when she spoke English and identified herself as an American, she also felt strongly that she was Chinese. As a teenager, she didn't expect any cultural problems when she visited her mother's family in a rural area of mainland China for the first time, but in fact, she was miserable, finding everything strange, from sleeping arrangements to the food to the family outhouse.

One of the ways that children come to feel part of the culture is by sharing in some of the common experiences of children growing up there. Going to school in the minority language home country will contribute tremendously to a child's feeling of belonging to the culture. Having cousins near the same age helps too, especially if they are willing to share knowledge about media, clothes, and social norms for their peers. Children want to fit in with

187

Chapter Twelve

other kids their age, so a visit to the home country involving contact with peers usually results in learning of both language and culture.

> **My daughter has the habit of kicking off her shoes** when she arrives at someone's home for a visit. This is what we do at our house, a custom that reflects a variety of cultural experiences; my husband's Iranian childhood, the decade he spent in Sweden, and the years I spent in Japan. It occasionally garners her puzzled looks here in the United States, though her American grandparents take it as an indication that she is happily making herself at home.

Parents may not be fully aware of all the changes that have taken place in their home country since they've been away, making it harder to prepare children. Those who've been living abroad for some time often find they're out-of-date. Their language is old-fashioned, and their knowledge of childhood in the home country may not be current, either. Parents who have been away for awhile may want to talk with their adult siblings, especially if they have children, too, about how things may have changed.

Sometimes parents are not very attentive to some of the differences between the two countries in how children behave and how adults interact with them, until they take their children on a visit to their home country. If one parent is not from the minority language culture, he or she may need some instruction, too. From typical bedtimes to the degree to which children are free to speak their minds, there can be significant differences in acceptable children's behavior and parenting practices. Unaware parents can be caught off-guard, as the Danish woman who made the mistake of leaving her baby in a baby carriage parked outside a New York City cafe (a common practice in Copenhagen) discovered when she was arrested. At the very least, parents will want to make sure they have instructed their children on the basics of polite behavior, especially in those areas where there is a significant difference from what is expected of children in their majority culture.

Chapter Thirteen

Special Situations
and Daily Dilemmas

Drawing on my fine command of the English language, I said nothing.
—Robert Benchley

Both day-to-day problems and more serious ones challenge parents' ability to continue with raising children bilingually. In this chapter we explore some of the more common issues that arise in the daily lives of bilingual families, as well as serious issues that affect some.

Chapter Thirteen

Special Situations

Death of a Parent

The death of a parent is a traumatic experience for a child. In bilingual families this bereavement is sometimes accompanied by the loss of contact with a language. When there are extended family and friends who speak the language of the parent who has died, they may be willing to help children continue with some use of the language, but the amount of time the children are exposed to it will decrease, with subsequent effects on the children's bilingual skills. If the lost language was the child's stronger language, the negative impact is exacerbated.

Divorce

Divorce can also result in the loss of a language, although the process may occur more slowly. When children spend less time with a parent who had provided most of their exposure to a language due to divorce, little by little, their proficiency in the language begins to erode. Especially when visits with the parent are intermittent and relatively brief, children may not have time to fully recover from the lack of use.

Learning Delays and Disabilities

When children are diagnosed with disabilities or learning delays, parents are sometimes advised to give up using one of the family's two languages with the child. This advice doesn't take into account the fact that for many families, raising the children bilingually is a necessity, rather than a choice. Families will need to modify their plans with regard to language, but it is sometimes still possible to continue with two languages. Of course, it depends in part on the type and severity of the diagnosis.

Special Situations and Daily Dilemmas

"In Grade 9, I was diagnosed with dyslexia. Actually, it is called dysgraphia. This is a form of dyslexia. It is a transference disability where I don't perceive what I read, and then I can't properly write down whatever I have in my thoughts. If it is verbal or if someone reads it to me, I can understand it a little bit better. When I found out about this, I figured, well, school was over. Had I come all this way in French immersion just to get to this point? Now what do I do? We brought in advisors from the school board. Along with the teachers, my Mom, and me, the advisors devised plans on how to learn. Now, learning was already tough for me as it was. Learning in French made it doubly tough, and now I had dyslexia. But, the French immersion program was incredible! The teachers were great. At this point, because every grade gets a little more difficult, I had a lot of problems reading. By Grade 9, I had begun to have all of my exams read on to audiocassette and taken in a separate room. I understood the exam, I understood the content, but I still had the problem of writing. Again, the school jumped in and said: 'Here is a laptop computer. Here is a teacher with some spare time and can write out what you are verbally telling them—the answers.' Within the next year, I noticed that my marks had dramatically risen."

—French immersion student, Edmonton, Canada

Being diagnosed with problems like dyslexia or Attention Deficit Disorder (ADD) doesn't mean the child can't succeed in learning two languages, although the family may need to modify their strategies. Families may be reluctant to push a child with dyslexia to learn to read in both languages, and given the diagnosis often comes when a child is quite late in learning to read, it may be important to focus on literacy skills in the majority language.

Even with more severe problems, decisions regarding language use should be made carefully. In cases of autism, for instance, if the parents have been using a minority language most of the time, with the assumption he or she will learn the majority language outside the home and at school, suddenly dropping the minority language could be harmful. The problem is compounded when the parents don't speak the majority language well. Parents will have to work extra hard at connecting with an autistic child, and trying to do it in a language they don't speak well is an extra burden.

Chapter Thirteen

In the case of a hearing impairment, having the child learn a sign language is usually recommended. Parents will want to consider the fact that if the child is expected to learn two spoken languages, in addition to signing they will need to support three languages under challenging conditions. In this case, dropping the child's weaker spoken language might be appropriate.

There are some problems that parents will be aware of from birth, such as when a child has Down Syndrome (DS). It is becoming clear that children with DS are capable of learning much more than used to be thought, with many participating in mainstream classrooms at school, learning to read and write, and in some cases, acquiring bilingual language skills.

Dr. Sue Buckley, Director of the Centre for Disability Studies at the University of Portsmouth, England, and Director of Research for the Down Syndrome Educational Trust states, "Where a family is naturally bilingual we encourage them to treat the child with Down Syndrome as they would other children in the family with regard to language exposure. We do encourage language and reading teaching to focus on the language the child will need for school and community, however. We base our advice on contact with successfully bilingual children."

Adoption and Language Loss

Parents who take older children through international adoption are sometimes concerned about the children suddenly losing contact with their first language. Children in this situation undergo a rather traumatic form of language attrition, loss of a language. It is common for these children not to speak for some time, which is not surprising given they have to hear the language before they make attempts to start using it. Parents who are concerned shouldn't delay in having their children tested, however. Depending on the child's care previous to the adoption, they may have experienced a lack of stimulation or nutritional deficits that could be causing problems in speech. Parents who want to mitigate the effects of the sudden language loss should be reassured there are many individuals who experience language attrition who go on to develop normal use of their second language. Providing plenty of language stimulation will help.

Special Situations and Daily Dilemmas

Daily Dilemmas

Problems with Relatives and Raising Bilingual Children

When one parent speaks the majority language, his or her extended family may be concerned about the decision to raise the children with two languages. Although the benefits of bilingualism are becoming better known, grandparents may not be current with the latest child development research, and may worry about language delays or confusion.

Bilingual grandparents, aunts and uncles will sometimes surprise parents who are working hard to expose their children to the family's minority language by speaking the majority language with them instead. In some cases, these relatives are the only opportunity the children will have to use the language outside of the immediate family. They may persist in using the majority language even after the parents ask them to use the minority language.

People who are bilingual will typically use the language that best facilitates communication in any given situation. When relatives estimate their use of the majority language is better than the children's use of the minority language, they may choose the majority language because they want to able to make a connection with them. This calculation is likely to be unconscious, and they may not even be aware they're choosing to speak the majority language with the children, especially if you and your spouse have asked them to use the other language.

Sometimes extended family members will choose the majority language in order to be polite to those who don't speak the minority language. When one parent doesn't speak the family's minority language at all, bilingual relatives from the other side of the family may feel it is rude to exclude that person from the conversation by using it.

Chapter Thirteen

One way to deal with this is for that parent to make a sincere effort to start learning the language, too. Even if relatives choose to use the majority language, asking questions about the minority language will bring it into the conversation, and make the additional point for the children that the language is valuable and interesting. The non-speaking parent could also try being absent some of the time, so that the conversation can flow without concerns about whether someone is being excluded. Young children often stick to their mothers, and if the mother only speaks the majority language, her presence may decrease the likelihood of children interacting in the minority language with others present.

Language use can reflect feelings of which people are not even aware. It is possible when bilingual speakers persist in using the majority language with children in a bilingual family they're being influenced by their perception of the children as being more a part of the majority language culture. They may be using the majority language as a way of bridging a perceived cultural gap and if you suspect this might be the case, try meeting them partway from the other side. Make sure children have some familiarity with the culture of their minority language. If it isn't possible to visit the home country, show pictures and tell stories.

Extended family members who are speakers of the minority language, especially monolingual speakers, may not be satisfied with the children's use of the language. This kind of reaction can be discouraging to both parents and children.

> "My wife and I spoke Japanese to our daughter for her first two years, but she didn't speak at all. The daycare center psychologist suggested I speak in English, since she heard English all day. She literally burst out speaking for the first time. The psychologist said she was probably confused since she only heard Japanese for 2-3 hours each evening. Later, she disliked Japanese because it wasn't cool."
>
> **—Sheridan Tatsuno, Aptos, California**

Special Situations and Daily Dilemmas

Using the Minority Language when Majority Language Speakers are Present

Parents who are trying to be consistent in their use of the family's minority language run up against a problem as their children enter school and make friends who only speak the majority language. Is it appropriate to use the minority language when you are driving the car pool? Should you use it with your daughter when she has friends over? Can you cheer your child in the minority language at sporting events?

There are a number of choices in how to deal with this. Some parents use the language they normally would, and then translate at least some part of it, so that the children's friends are not left out. Some modify their language practice, depending on the place and the people present. One could speak the minority language when actually at home, regardless of who is there, translating when necessary, but switch to the majority language while at school or extracurricular events. Asking the children about their preferences and their friends' comfort is another possibility.

Maintaining Minority Languages as Children Grow Older

As children grow older, they often speak the family's minority language with increasing reluctance. It is difficult to keep them motivated in the face of all the other interests and responsibilities competing for their time. As adults, many of these same children who grew up with bilingual parents, but don't speak their family's minority language, regret that fact and wish their parents had been more insistent they learn the language. (This is no doubt irritating to their parents, who remember the indifference or even dislike children had for learning the language at the time.)

Chapter Thirteen

Once in school, children are likely to become concerned about seeming too different from their peers, and this can cause them to avoid speaking their family's minority language. Children also start to have their own interests and become involved in their own activities as they get older. This can affect their use of the family's minority language because they are spending less time with the family. A teenager with a part-time job, band or sports practice, and friends, is less likely to be around for family dinner and the conversation in the family's minority language that goes with it. Older children may also want to drop Saturday school or other enrichment activities intended to foster learning of the family's minority language, even if they were previously enthusiastic about them, when those activities conflict with their current interests. Teenagers and even pre-teens may also use rejection of the family's minority language as a way of establishing independence from the family.

The tactics parents use to counter these developments will vary depending on the family's resources and parenting styles. Some families will start planning an overseas trip for a motivational boost. Some increase the number of enrichment resources such as CD-ROMs available for the children to use. Others bring out the kitty jar for family members to feed when they slip into the wrong language for a given situation. Some parents will lose their temper, or give up in disgust and disappointment.

With many teens, the more you insist they use the family's minority language, the further they'll dig in their heels. Some parents will react by becoming even firmer in requiring that children use the minority language. Not responding until the child uses the appropriate language is probably more effective than getting angry or threatening punishing consequences. However, refusing to respond is more likely to work if they feel they actually need you to respond, or do something for them. Teens who can manage their own transportation, food, and would prefer to be left alone anyway, may not respond to these tactics.

Special Situations and Daily Dilemmas

Once children have reached the teen years, parents may decide that the language has probably been established to the point that if the child takes a break from speaking it, he or she will be able to pick it up again later if they have a mind to do so. Arguments that can lead to resentment of the minority language might not seem worthwhile. Continuing to speak to the children in the minority language, but not reacting too much if they choose to speak the other language may work as a strategy in language maintenance for these parents. Teens who complain about the parent continuing to use the minority language can be told that if they have to the right to choose which language to speak, then so do you.

Some parents do find themselves in a no-win situation at this time. If you have a child who is embarrassed to have friends hear the parent use the minority language, and who is also embarrassed by the fact that the parent doesn't sound like a native speaker in the majority language, being in public places with the child can be extremely difficult. Languages which are not considered prestige languages in the greater community are more likely to provoke this reaction in children, but it can happen with any language. To be a teen is often to be painfully self-conscious, so children may be embarrassed to have a parent speaking even a language with relatively high prestige in his or her majority language community. Parents are sometimes surprised to have their children react this way when they previously seemed proud of their minority language, or if it is one that the children's friends may even be studying at school.

Chapter Thirteen

If you have been able to provide your child with real world links and contacts to other people who use the same language, whether adults outside the family or peers, children may be willing to speak the language with them even if they are reluctant to do so with you. Going abroad to visit their cousins is appealing to many teens, especially if they can go alone or perhaps go earlier or stay longer than the rest of the family. Family trips may be more motivating for older children if they are allowed some input into what the family will do in the home country.

It is a good idea to encourage children to pursue some individual interests in the minority language culture. Look for magazines on cars, computers or fashion in your family's minority language. Seek out coaches or instructors for extracurricular activities who speak the language. If there is a martial arts instructor who speaks Chinese, Korean, or French, maybe it's worth driving across town to have your twelve-year-old study with that person. If your teen-aged son or daughter decides to create a Pan-Asian pop band with a few friends, maybe they could practice in the garage.

This strategy is more likely to be successful when the child initiates the activity, but sometimes parents can get away with pointing out an opportunity that coincides with their child's interests, that just happens to require some use of the family's minority language. Teens interested in volunteering, or who are required to do it as part of their education, might choose to help out in a soup kitchen, senior center, or refugee organization that serves an ethnic community with some speakers of their minority language. Schools with language programs often welcome volunteers, too.

Pre-teens who are still spending a lot of time at home may enjoy some new media in the family's minority language. This could be a good time for families to buy some new computer games, seek out a new source for videos and DVDs in the language, or even invest in cable, if programming in your minority language is available. Summer language camps are another possibility for giving your child's minority language a boost. They may be more interested in attending if a friend also plans to go.

Chapter Fourteen

An Afterword on Measuring Success

*"It usually takes more than three weeks
to prepare a good impromptu speech. "*
— **Mark Twain**

Making the decision to raise children with two languages requires thought and careful planning for success, especially in a monolingual environment. How does one know if one has succeeded? The most important measure of success in raising bilingual children is whether the children are happy, and the degree of satisfaction parents feel with their children's language development.

Whether parents are satisfied is going to depend in part on how realistic their goals are, and the amount of support they are able to find for the family's two languages both within and outside the family. Parents who are bothered by a foreign-sounding accent or who will be unhappy their children are not indistinguishable from native speakers of the minority language will need to invest more in supporting their children's bilingualism than parents who are satisfied with mostly receptive skills. On the other hand, there are parents who will be happy with their children's bilingualism, even if the chil-

Chapter Fourteen

dren's skills in one language are relatively weak, because they recognize their children have accomplished something special, perhaps under circumstances that were not the best ones for learning two languages. Parents should also remember their children's language use and proficiency can change over time and if a child's skills in one language are much weaker than the other, and parents view this as a problem, they can take steps to provide more exposure and opportunities to use the language.

It is important that parents use both languages in contexts that are meaningful to children, are consistent in their use, and persist in providing exposure to both languages despite changes over time in the family's circumstances. The opportunity to acquire an additional language is a gift parents can share with their children, and like all gifts, should be carefully chosen and given.

I hope the information in this book and the experience of other bilingual families, shared here, help you create a plan for bilingual family life for your own unique bilingual family.

Appendices

Appendix A

Resources for Bilingual Families

Bilingual Family Newsletter edited by Marjukka Grover, from Multilingual Matters. Articles, family profiles, interviews, tips, suggestions and a question column.

To subscribe contact: Multilingual Matters
Frankfurt Lodge, Clevedon Hall, Victoria Road
Clevedon, England BS21 7HH
Tel: +44 (0)1275-876519
Fax: +44 (0) 1275-871673

Center for Applied Linguistics (CAL)
4646 40th Street, NW
Washington, DC 20016-1859
Ph: (202)362-0700
Fax: (202)362-3740
www.cal.org

The Center for Applied Linguistics (CAL) is a nonprofit organization that directs research, disseminates information, provides teacher training, and produces materials on issues related to language and culture. The organization's mission is to improve communication through a better understanding of language and culture. Their services are aimed primarily at teachers and other language professionals, but there is much that parents in bilingual families will find useful, including information on subjects like bilingual education, literacy in a second language, and foreign languages. CAL also has a number of searchable databases available on its website for families looking for language programs or materials.

Appendices

**Center for Multilingual Multicultural Research
at the University of Southern California**
www.usc.edu/dept/education/CMMR/home.html
Research at the center is in the area of multilingual education, and will be mostly of interest to educators and other language professionals. However, visitors to the center website will find links to Asian-Pacific Island, Latino-Hispanic, Native American-American Indian, African-American, and Bilingual/ESL/Multilingual Education resources by checking the site index.

European Bureau for Lesser Used Languages
Rue Saint-Josse, 49 B-1210 Bruxelles
Tel: +32 2 218.25.90 Fax: +32 2 218.19.74
www.eblul.org
This organization advocates for speakers of minority languages in the European Union and is a good source of information on less commonly spoken languages in the European Union. The English/French website includes a database of language-related organizations, information on funding of language education projects in the EU, and a section called Web of Words with information on minority languages in Europe.

Intercultural Development Research Association (IDRA)
5835 Callaghan Road, Suite 350
San Antonio, Texas 78228-1190
Ph: (210)444-1710
Fax: (210)444-1714
www.idra.org
The nonprofit Intercultural Development Research Association advocates for equitable education for language minority students through support of bilingual education. IDRA supports a number of valuable projects such as the Bilingual Education Collaborating Alliance (BECA), a three-year program to alleviate the severe shortage of bilingual education and English as a Second Language (ESL) teachers in Texas. Parents can contact IDRA for information on bilingual education, and the education rights of language minority children.

Appendices

National Association for Bilingual Education (NABE)
1030 15th Street, NW, Suite 470
Washington, DC 2005-1503
Ph: (202)898-1829
Fax: (202)789-2866
www.nabe.org
A national nonprofit organization based in Washington, D.C., NABE promotes excellence and equity in education by representing the interests of language minority students and professionals in bilingual education. Another good resource for parents with general questions about bilingual education and their children's education rights.

Appendix B

Internet Resources

I strongly recommend an Internet connection as an investment for bilingual families. According to Global Reach, a global marketing consulting business, a little over 35% of all Internet users went on-line in English in 2002. Other languages frequently used on-line include Chinese, Japanese, Spanish, and German. Even if the home country where your family's minority language is spoken is not particularly well connected, it is often easier to find books and other products in minority languages online than in local bookstores.

The Internet can provide older children and teens with the ability to participate in an online community of peers and to explore the culture of the home country of a family's minority language. For adults in the household, having an Internet connection may allow them to listen to radio, view video, and read news from their home country.

The Internet can facilitate communication with relatives and friends who are far away. (At our house we've set up a webcam and microphone, so we can wave and shout at our relatives in Iran!) Bilingual families can also find online communities of other families who are raising children in two languages, and share some of the same interests and concerns.

Appendices

If it is not possible for you to have an Internet connection at home, check with your local library. In the United States it is now the norm for libraries to provide Internet access to the general public. In the U.S. and other countries, Internet cafes where people pay to go online are available in many places.

Some common abbreviations used online related to family bilingualism are OPOL (one person—one language), ML for majority language, and ml for minority language.

The websites listed here use English primarily unless otherwise noted.

Internet Communities for Bilingual Families

Bilingual Families Web Page
http://www.nethelp.no/cindy/biling-fam.html
This is a good place to start your explorations on the web. Cindy Kandolf provides basic information for bilingual families, including a list of common myths about bilingualism, an overview of the politics surrounding the issue, and information on other resources for bilingual families. She also hosts the bilingual families mailing list. Discussion on the very active list covers a wide range of topics, from the history of bilingualism among the aristocracy in Imperial Russia to why someone's computer keeps crashing when the kids play their latest game from Japan. It is a nice way for parents to communicate with other parents who may have similar interests and issues, but can quickly fill your email inbox. Subscribers who don't want to read or delete 30-50 posts a day should choose the 'lite' version of the list.

The Bilingual Pages
http://www.angelfire.com/ut/henrikholm/bilingual/bilingual01.html
This friendly website is created by and for bilingual families. It hosts a "Multilingual Family Café" with regular scheduled chat sessions for members. Visitors will also find recipes, tongue twisters in many languages, and links to personal webpages of other bilingual families. By subscribing to the Bilingual Families Web Page (see previous website) you can access archived discussion threads organized into categories of frequently asked questions.

Appendices

Chanpon
http://www.chanpon.org
Chanpon means "a mixture of disparate things" in Japanese. Chanpon.org is an organization and website providing a discussion space and resources on topics such as raising bicultural children, professional networking, and Japan-US relations. The group was initiated by former students at several international schools in Tokyo, who wanted to connect with others who have had similar experiences of growing up with Japanese and another culture.

Enfants Bilingues
http://www.enfantsbilingues.com/
This website for bilingual families in French gives an overview of family bilingualism, along with links to articles and other resources. Includes a forum.

Foreign Wives Club
www.foreignwivesclub.com
An online community of women in bicultural marriages.

Imausland
http://www.imausland.org/
You can look for other Germans in your area at this site, designed for Germans abroad.

The International Couples' Homepage
www.geocities.com/Heartland/4448/Couples.html
The design of this Geocities site is a little chaotic, but fun. Available in 13 languages, it includes a list of couples of different nationalities interested in communicating with others in similar relationships. There is also a nice list of resources on bilingualism and multilingualism, and a chat room.

Appendices

Kids Bilingual Network
http://hjem.wanadoo.dk/~wan42942/frameset.html
Designed to help families meet other families in their area using the same language(s). Parents submit a short description about themselves and their families, along with contact information. Some pages on the site are available in German and Danish.

Other Internet Resources

Ask a Linguist
www.linguistlist.org/~ask-ling/index.html
Concerned about your kids mixing their two languages? Don't know if it's a good time to add a third language? Ask a professional linguist! Responses come from a panel of language professionals, mostly academics in linguistics at universities in the United States and Great Britain.

Barahona Center for the Study of Books
in Spanish for Children and Adolescents
http://www.csusm.edu/csb
Provided by the Barahona Center at California State University in San Marcos, this English/Spanish website is an excellent resource for parents who want to boost their children's literacy skills in Spanish. Parents will find a well-designed, searchable database of recommended books in Spanish for children and teenagers, and a smaller database of books in English about Latinos and Latino culture. Click on Lists/Listados to check out lists of recorded Spanish books and singalongs, magazines for children and teenagers in Spanish with publisher contact information, and winners of the prestigious Newbery and Caldecott medals that have been translated into Spanish.

BBC World Service
http://www.bbc.co.uk/worldservice
Listen to news in 43 languages. Programming includes current events, entertainment, science news, and English lessons presented in each language.

Appendices

Bilingual Parenting in a Foreign Language
www.byu.edu/~bilingua/index.html
This website is for parents who are interested in raising their children using a foreign language; that is, one that neither parent speaks natively. Lists of resources such as books and articles related to bilingual parenting and children's language development, and where to find books and software for children in a variety of languages.

China Sprout
www.chinasprout.com
This is also a shopping site, with products aimed at bicultural families and families who have adopted children from China, but the website has so many other features that I've included it here. There are bulletin boards on topics like biculturalism, biracial families, bilingualism, and Chinese language. When I last visited there was extensive discussion of language delays in adopted children. There are also a number of interesting essays on the guest column page by parents writing about their experiences raising bilingual and bicultural children.

Educational Resources Information Center (ERIC)
Ph:1-800-538-3742 (1-800-LET-ERIC)
http://ericir.syr.edu
Huge website devoted to information on education and related topics, including parenting and bilingualism. Includes a searchable database of resources, and a feature called "Ask an ERIC expert."

The Library in the Sky
www.nwrel.org/sky
From the Northwest Regional Educational Library, collections of educational websites organized by subject. Start with the English as a Second Language (ESL) or Foreign Language Departments to explore link collections on specific languages, or on topics such as bilingual education.

Appendices

**Massachusetts Institute of Technology Library Guide
to Foreign Language News**
www.libraries.mit.edu/guides/types/flnews
This on-line guide from the Massachusetts Institute of Technology (MIT) provides links to on-line newspapers, magazines and journals in a variety of languages.

Multilingual Songbook
www.laukart.de/multisite
The Multilingual Songbook site features lyrics to children's songs in 25 languages, although the selection in non-European languages is limited. Music is available for some songs.

Sprachhexen
www.sprachhexen.com
Attractive website aimed at bilingual families who speak German. Includes a forum, a subscription newsletter, and a list of German language playgroups, mostly in the U.S., but with a growing international list. Visitors can shop for books, videos, and games. There is a useful "Tips" section with information on how to get German TV, video and DVD systems, resource links, and more. An English version for families who use English as a minority language is under construction at this writing at:**www.sprachhexen.com/englisch**

UCLA Language Materials Project
www.lmp.ucla.edu
This on-line database provides information on materials for teaching less commonly taught languages. The database includes resources for the teaching and learning of over 100 languages. It is designed to allow searchers to target particular varieties of some languages, such as Arabic or Chinese, and also proficiency level (beginning, intermediate or advanced.) The majority of materials listed are aimed at adults, but if you are looking and having trouble finding materials in languages like Amharic, Catalan, Estonian, or Shona, this is a good place to start.

Appendices

Zona Europa
www.zonaeuropa.com
Check out the periodical listings here to find car/motorcycle/computer/music/ fashion magazines in your family's European minority language for your teen.

Zona Latina
www.zonalatina.com
This sister site to Zona Europa provides information on Latin American media and marketing. Most useful to bilingual families are the links to Spanish language television stations and schedules, radio, newspapers, and magazines in Latin America, the USA, and Europe.

Educational Resources on the Internet

The resources in this section will be most useful for families who are trying to provide some academic support for their children's minority language at home.

Asian Studies WWW Virtual Library
http://coombs.anu.edu.au/WWWVL-AsianStudies.html
Produced by the Australian National University, this site provides a wealth of links to other websites related to an extensive number of regions and countries in Asia, including the Middle East, the former Soviet states, and the Pacific. Good starting point whether you are looking for economic or geographic information, language links, or virtual art galleries.

BBC Language Page
http://www.bbc.co.uk/education/languages
Information on who speaks what where, as well as online lessons in Spanish, French, German, and English. There are also learning activities in Welsh, Scots Gaelic, and Irish, and entertaining pages where readers share their language blunders and learning tips.

Appendices

California Language Teachers Association Foreign Language Lessons
www.clta.net/lessons
Nice collection of web-based foreign language lessons. There are four levels of Spanish lessons, and three levels of French. Other languages include Chinese, German, Japanese, and Tagalog.

Discovery School Guide for Educators:
World Geography, Languages and Regional Information
http://school.discovery.com/schrockguide/world/worldrw.html
From Discovery.com, Kathy Schrock's Guide for Educators is useful for parents and older children, too. You'll find links to general languages learning sites as well as some organized by specific language or region.

ePALS
www.epals.com
ePALS Classroom Exchange is an online K-12 classroom network. Teachers or homeschooling parents can list their group's profile on the site, or search other profiles for appropriate penpals to correspond with via email. Unlike many penpal websites, ePals does not list individual profiles or photos, and offers monitoring of email exchanges to ensure children's safety. The website is available in English, Spanish, French, Portuguese, German and Japanese.

JapaneseOnline.com
http://www.japanese-online.com/
Online Japanese lessons, interesting links collection and an active forum of Japanese language learners and others with an interest in Japan. Also a math challenge: story problems given to Japanese junior high school students during placement tests. Problems are translated into English. Provided by Pacific Software Publishing, Inc.

Appendix C

Shopping: Toys, Books, Games, DVDs and Videos for Bilingual Children

I've given product information for the companies below in order to give you a general sense of the kinds of products that are available from each company. Obviously, the products that companies will actually have in stock at the time you contact them may differ from what I've listed here. Many of these companies have websites with features in addition to shopping, including forums, playgroups lists, or links to articles likely to be of interest to website visitors interested in children's language development. Because many of these companies are trying to reach multilingual, multicultural consumers across the globe, some operate primarily online.

Amazon
www.amazon.com

Amazon offers books, music, videos, DVDs, computer games in English, Spanish, French, German, and Japanese through a family of websites in seven countries. On the Amazon home page, choose International from the menu to access the various country sites. For parents in the United States looking for Spanish language products, you can access a menu from the International Page that will probably be easier to use than the regular search engine on the U.S. website, unless you know the title of a book or video already. The Canadian site is bilingual English/French, helpful for parents who don't speak French, but whose children are learning it at school.

Appendices

Asia for Kids
4480 Lake Forest Dr. #302 Cincinnati, Ohio 45242 USA
Phone orders: 1-800-888-9681
To request a print catalogue 1-800-765-5885 or 1-513-563-3100 (from outside
of the United States) Monday - Friday: 9 a.m. - 5 p.m. Eastern Standard Time
www.afk.com
Asia for Kids carries an extensive selection of items including books, software,
videos, CDs and cassettes, dolls, games, posters, crafts. Materials are offered
in many Asian languages, including languages from the Middle East, as well
as English, French and Spanish. Nice selection of dolls, including Yue-Sai dolls
(Barbie alternative), Asian Corelle baby dolls, and multicultural soft dolls. The
company website includes an adoption resource corner, and information on a
number of Asian festivals.

The Bess Press, Inc.
3565 Harding Ave. Honolulu, HI 96816 USA
Tel: 808-734-7159
www.besspress.com
Independent Hawaiian publisher with illustrated word books for children in a
number of Asian and Pacific languages, including Japanese, Korean, Samoan,
and Chamorro.

Books Without Borders
13509 NE 93rd Street, Redmond, WA 98052-6417
Tel: 1-888-840-BWOB (2962)
Fax: 1-425-828-7790
www.bookswithoutborders.com
This Internet bookstore features children's books, audiocassettes, and videos
in Chinese, English, French, German, Italian, Russian, and Spanish, along
with some bilingual products. Multilingual Disney Read-along DVDs are a
popular item.

Appendices

Celebrate the Child

1821 Commercial Dr. "S"

Harvey, LA 70058

Tel: 1-888-223-5278 (Toll free)

www.celebratechild.com

Online store primarily aimed at families in the USA who have adopted internationally, but they do carry some language items. Online catalog is searchable either by product type (language, music, books) or by culture/area (Cambodia, China, Korea, Latin America, Russia, Vietnam.) This is a good place to find special toys or gifts, such as handmade dolls from Guatamala, inexpensive Matryoshka nesting dolls, or traditional clothing from Russia or Korea. Some books for adults, and special products related to adoption, such as adoption announcements.

China Books & Periodicals, Inc.

www.chinabooks.com

Phone: 415-282-2994

2929 24th Street San Francisco, CA 94110 USA

Distributor of books and other products related to China, including Chinese books, tapes, and games for children. Many of the items are not pictured in the online catalog, but you can request a print catalog by mail, phone, or via the website.

Heritage Source

P.O. Box 802542 Santa Clarita, CA 91380-2542 USA

Tel: (661) 263-0623 Toll free (877) 758-0137

Fax: (661) 263-7703

www.heritagesource.com

Carolyn Sanwo was inspired to start her online bookstore when she had difficulty finding books related to her Japanese-American heritage to share with her two daughters. The website features Japanese and Japanese-American books for children and adults in English with a thoughtful selection of picture books, fiction and non-fiction for young adults. Special orders and search requests for out of print books welcome. No print catalogue currently available.

Appendices

Lee & Low Books
1-888-320-3395 (Toll free)
95 Madison Ave., Ste. 606, New York, NY 10016 USA
www.leeandlow.com
Lee and Low is an independent publisher of children's books emphasizing stories about multicultural children in contemporary settings. Most books are in English, with some available in Spanish and Chinese. Books from Lee and Low have won numerous awards, and their website has a number of interesting links for parents interested in multicultural literature.

Milet Books
6 North End Parade, London W14 0SJ England
Tel +44 20 7603 5477 Fax +44 20 7610 5475
www.milet.com
Publisher of beautifully illustrated multicultural and dual language (bilingual) books for children in many languages.

Multicultural Books and Videos, Inc.
12033 St. Thomas Crescent Tecumseh, Ontario, CANADA N8N 3V6
28880 Southfield Road, Suite 183 Lathrup Village, MI 48076 USA
Tel: 800-567-2220 (Toll free: Canada & USA)
Fax: Canada (519) 735-5043 USA (810) 559-2465
www.multiculbv.com
This company has an especially good selection of films from India. They also carry bilingual dictionaries and illustrated dictionaries for children in languages a variety of languages, such as Czech, Farsi (Persian), and Japanese. Other items include translations of Dr. Seuess, Robert Munsch, Disney and Asterix. There are some teaching guides for children's films (mostly Disney in Spanish and French) with suggestions for activities related to the videos. The on-line catalog can be difficult to navigate, and the search function doesn't always turn up products that are, in fact, there. Company representatives are very helpful by phone, though.

Appendices

Multicultural Kids
Tel: 1-800-711-2321 (Toll free)
P.O. Box 757 Palatine, Illinois 60078-0757 USA
www.multiculturalkids.com
Great place to look for fun, unusual toys such as stamp sets of Celtic or Western African symbols, Chinese characters or the Hebrew alphabet, or puzzles of maps of China. Good selection of dolls, including Language Littles, who speak French, Spanish, Italian or Chinese, and Yue-Sai fashion dolls. Also carries music, craft projects and electronic dictionaries in a variety of languages, including some especially designed for children. No print catalogue currently available.

Oui for Kids
www.ouiforkids.com
On-line store, located in New Brunswick, Canada, created by the mother of a child in a French immersion program. Online catalog includes picture books, and a good selection of book for older children and teens, including translations of high interest classics like The Wizard of Oz, Dracula, Frankenstein, and Little Women. Software selections include Caillou, Mia, Scooby Doo, Harry Potter, Arthur and TinTin. No print catalogue available.

Small Fry Productions
1200 Alpha Drive, Suite B Alpharetta, GA 30004 USA
Tel: 1-800-521-5311 (Toll free)
www.small-fry.com
This company produces educational videos, including a Bilingual Baby series of language videos for infants and toddlers. You can order online or call to request a print catalogue.

Appendices

Teacher's Discovery Outlet Store
2741 Paldan Dr., Auburn Hills, Mi 48326 USA
Tel: 1-800-832-2437 (Toll free) Fax: 248-340-7212
www.teachersdiscovery.com
Small, eclectic selection of language learning materials in Spanish, French and German. Good deals on flashcards and games. Free, downloadable comprehension quizzes from the website (mostly in English) about a variety of foreign language videos.

World of Reading
P.O. Box 13092 Atlanta, Georgia 30324-0092 USA
Tel: (404) 233-4042 Toll free (800) 729-3703
Fax: (404) 237-5511
www.wor.com
Large selection of books, music, computer software, videos, and DVDs for children and adults in many languages.

Appendix D

Biculturalism

Recommended Books

Picture Books

All the Colors We Are: The Story of How We Get Our Skin Color by Katie Kissinger, photos by Wernher Krutein. Pub: Redleaf Press.
> Attractive non-fiction book that explains how melanin affects the color of our skin, also impact of the sun, the role of heredity in determining our skin's color.

El Chino by Allen Say. Pub: Houghton Mifflin.
> Beautifully illustrated book tells the true story of Billy Wong, the first Chinese-American bullfighter.

Appendices

<u>Jalepeno Bagels</u> by Natasha Wing, illustrated by Robert Casilla. Pub: Antheum Books.
   For International Day at his school, Pablo wants to bring something from his family's bakery that will reflect his family's blended Jewish-Mexican culture.

<u>Halmoni and The Picnic</u> by Sook-Nyul Choi, illustrated by Karen Dugan. Pub: Houghton Mifflin.
   Yunmi's grandmother has recently come from Korea to live in the United States. When she decides to come on a school picnic, Yunmi is afraid her classmates will make fun her traditional food and clothing.

<u>How My Family Lives in America</u> by Susan Kuklin. Pub: Simon and Schuster.
   Three American kindergartners reflect on their families' unique multicultural heritages. Their comments are natural and realistic, as are the photographic illustrations.

<u>How My Parents Learned to Eat</u> by Ina R. Friedman, illustrated by Allen Say. Pub: Houghton Mifflin.
   Charming story of how a little girl's American father and Japanese mother met in Japan. Some may be bothered by the somewhat dated presentation of Japanese life.

<u>I Hate English!</u> By Ellen Levine, illustrated by Steve Bjorkman. Pub: Bt Bound.
   Mei Mei has moved from Hong Kong to New York City with her family, and fears losing her identity as she adjusts to American culture and learns English.

<u>Margaret and Margarita</u> by Lynn Reiser. Pub: Greenwillow.
   Simple bilingual story about an English-speaking girl and a Spanish-speaking girl who realize they have much in common despite their language differences.

Appendices

<u>Tea with Milk</u> by Allen Say. Pub: Houghton Mifflin.
May has grown up in the United States and is resentful after she graduates from high school when her parents decide the family will return to Japan.

<u>Ugly Vegetables</u> by Grace Lin. Pub: Charlesbridge.
A little girl is disappointed with her family's garden when her mother insists on planting ugly Chinese vegetables, instead of pretty flowers like the neighbors.

<u>Yoko</u> by Rosemary Wells. Pub: Hyperion Press.
A little kitten named Yoko is embarrassed when classmates tease her about her sushi lunch, and things get even worse when her teacher tries to help her by planning an International Food Day. Fortunately, Timmy the raccoon is so hungry he'll even try sushi.

Appropriate for teens

<u>Esperanza Rising</u> by Pam Munoz Ryan. Pub: Scholastic.
Historical novel based on the life of the author's grandmother, in which a wealthy Mexican girl is forced to work as a laborer in a Depression-era migrant camp in California after her father's death.

<u>Walk Two Moons</u> by Sharon Creech. Pub: HarperCollins.
Lyrical, complex coming of age story, in which the main character's pride in her American Indian heritage is a source of strength.

<u>When I was Puerto Rican</u> by Esmeralda Santiago. Pub: Vintage Books.
A memoir of the author's childhood in poverty in 1950s Puerto Rico, and her difficult transition after moving to New York City. Also available in Spanish.

<u>Half and Half: Writers on Growing Up Biracial and Bicultural</u> edited by Claudine O'Hearn. Pub: Pantheon Books.
Thought-provoking collection of essays; comical, poignant and moving.

Appendices

<u>Yell-Oh Girls! Emerging Voices Explore Culture, Identity and Growing Up
Asian-American</u> edited by Vicki Nam. Pub: Quill.
Young Asian-American women write on issues such as body image, racism,
and dual identity.

<u>Who Are You? Voices of Mixed-Race Young People</u> edited by Pearl Fuyo
Gaskins. Pub: Henry Holt.
Young writers on growing up as a person of mixed race in American. Essays
and poetry.

Mostly for Parents

<u>Intercultural Marriage</u>, by Dugan Romano. Pub: Nicholas Brealey/Intercultural
Press.
Make sure to get the second edition, published in 2001, as it has an
expanded chapter on raising bicultural children, as well as new material on
dealing with divorce or death in bicultural marriages.

<u>The New Press Guide to Multicultural Resources for Young Readers </u>edited by
Daphne Muse. Pub: New Press.
This book is one parents may want to look for at the library, rather than
purchase, as it is expensive and more of a reference book. Reviews
approximately 1000 books with multicultural themes for children; includes
cautions on some books, essays on topics related to multicultural literature
and education.

Appendices

Films of Interest

These independent documentary films on topics related to cultural identity are off the beaten track, but well worth viewing, especially for teens wrestling with identity issues. Check your public library, or local university.

Tiger's Apprentice (1998) 57 minutes and _Xichlo(Cyclo)_ (1996) 21 minutes, both documentaries by Vietnamese-American independent filmmaker M. Trinh Nguyen. _Xichlo_ is the story of Nguyen's first visit to Saigon after emigrating to the United States. In _Tiger's Apprentice_ Nguyen returns to Vietnam, this time to document her great-uncle's practice of traditional medicine, of which she is initially highly skeptical. Nguyen explores her own bicultural identity as well as her former homeland. The films are in English and Vietnamese, with subtitles. Appropriate for teens, adults. For information contact Taro Root Films, 22-D Hollywood Avenue, Ho-Ho-Kus, New Jersey, 07423 USA **www.tarorootfilms.com**

That's a Family 35 minutes, directed by Debra Chasnoff for Women's Educational Media. This short film for children in elementary school features children of the same age talking about their non-traditional families, including multiracial and multicultural families, and those with gay and lesbian parents. Appropriate for elementary school aged children. For information contact Women's Educational Media, 2180 Bryant Street, Ste. 203, San Francisco, California 94110 USA. Tel: 415-641-4616 Fax: 415-641-4632 **www.womedia.org**

Yidl in the Middle: Growing Up Jewish in Iowa (1999) 56 minutes, a sometimes funny documentary memoir of filmmaker Marlene Booth's childhood, incorporating interviews, home movies, even a trip to Ms. Booth's high school reunion. Best for teens and adults.
For information contact New Day Films, 190 Route 17M, P.O. Box 1084, Harriman, New York 10926 USA Tel: (888) 367-9154 Fax: (201) 652-1973 **www.newday.com**

Appendix E

Some General Information on Languages

A language is a dialect with an army and a navy.
—Max Weinreich

Facts and figures regarding language and language use are necessarily imprecise but for those of us interested in language, a lot of fun. This appendix contains some general information on languages, which may be of interest to bilingual families, such as what languages have the highest numbers of speakers, which languages other than English are likely to be spoken at home in the United States, along with information on languages with relatively few speakers.

Living languages change constantly, and the way people use them also changes. Estimates from different sources regarding the number of speakers of different languages vary widely. Aside from the impossibility of accurately counting each and every speaker, decisions about who should be considered a "speaker" of a language differ as well. Some language surveys count native speakers only, while others count both native speakers and those who speak a language as a second language. Such surveys often rely on self-reporting, which may be inaccurate, as some people will overestimate their use of a language while others underestimate.

When one thinks of the degree of influence a language has, one must consider the geographic distribution of a language, in addition to the numbers of speakers. Some languages, such as Marathi, in India, have many native speakers, but are located in one country. Others, such as French, serve as an important tool for regional and global communication. The following table of the twenty most widely spoken languages in the world gives estimates of the number of native speakers of each language, although some speakers may be bilingual.

Appendices

The Twenty Most Widely Spoken Languages in the World

Language	Estimated Number of Speakers in Millions	Selected List of Countries in which the Language is Spoken
1. Chinese (Mandarin, Cantonese, Wu, Min and other varieties)	1,212	Brunei, Cambodia, China, Indonesia, Malaysia, Mongolia, Philippines, Singapore, South Africa, Taiwan, Thailand, Vietnam
2. Arabic	422	Algeria, Egypt, Iraq, Israel, Jordan, Kuwait, Lebanon, Libya, Morocco, Saudi Arabia, Sudan, Syria, Tunisia, UAE, Yemen
3. Hindi/Urdu	366	Afghanistan, India, Mauritius, Nepal, Pakistan Singapore, S. Africa, Thailand, Uganda
4. English	341	Australia, Botswana, Brunei, Cameroon, Canada, Eritrea, Ethiopia, Fiji, The Gambia, Guyana, India, Ireland, Israel, Lesotho, Liberia, Malaysia, Micronesia, Namibia, Nauru, New Zealand, Palau, Papua New Guinea, Samoa, Seychelles, Sierra Leone, Singapore, Solomon Islands, Somalia, S. Africa, Suriname, Swaziland, Tonga, U.K., U.S., Vanuatu, Zimbabwe, various Caribbean states
5. Spanish	322	Andorra, Argentina, Belize, Bolivia, Chile, Colombia, Costa Rica, Cuba, Dominican Rep., Ecuador, El Salvador, Equatorial Guinea, Guatemala, Honduras, Mexico, Morocco, Nicaragua, Panama, Paraguay, Peru, Spain, Uruguay, U.S., Venezuela
6. Bengali	207	Bangladesh, India, Singapore
7. Portuguese	176	Angola, Brazil, Cape Verde, France, Guinea-Bissau, Mozambique, Portugal, São Tomé and Príncipe
8. Russian	167	China, Israel, Mongolia, Russia, U.S.
9. Japanese	125	Japan, Singapore, Taiwan
10. German	100	Austria, Belgium, Bolivia, Czech Rep., Denmark, Germany, Hungary, Italy, Kazakhstan, Liechtenstein, Luxembourg, Paraguay, Poland, Romania, Slovakia, Switzerland
11. French	78	Algeria, Andorra, Belgium, Benin, Burkina Faso, Burundi, Cambodia, Cameroon, Canada, Chad, Democratic Republic of the Congo, Djibouti, France, Gabon, Guinea, Haiti, Ivory Coast, Laos, Luxembourg, Madagascar, Mali, Mauritania, Monaco, Morocco, Niger, Rwanda, Senegal, Seychelles, Switzerland, Togo, Tunisia, Vanuatu, Vietnam
12. Korean	78	China, Japan, N. Korea, S. Korea, Singapore, United States
13. Javanese	75	Indonesia, Malaysia, Singapore
14. Telugu	69	Fiji, India, Singapore
15. Marathi	68	India

Appendices

The Twenty Most Widely Spoken Languages in the World

Language	Estimated Number of Speakers in Millions	Selected List of Countries in which the Language is Spoken
16. Vietnamese	68	Cambodia, Canada, China Laos, United States, Vietnam
17. Tamil	66	India, Malaysia, Mauritius, Singapore, S. Africa, Sri Lanka
18. Italian	62	Croatia, Eritrea, France, Italy, San Marino, Slovenia, Switzerland
19. Turkish	61	Bulgaria, Cyprus, Greece, Macedonia, Romania, Turkey, Uzbekistan
20. Punjabi	57	Afghanistan, India, Pakistan

Data Sources: Ethnologue 14th Edition, Encarta

Geographic Distribution of Languages

Americans think of Europe as being a multilingual place, where bilingualism thrives, so it may be a surprise to learn that only 3% of the world's living languages are used there. Of course, many of the world's living languages have only a few speakers, such as Mara, a language of the indigenous people of Australia, which at last count had only 15 speakers. Just in the Republic of Vanuatu, a group of islands in the southwestern Pacific with an estimated population of 196,178, there are 109 languages currently in use.

Data Source: Ethnologue 14th Edition

The World's Living Languages in 2000

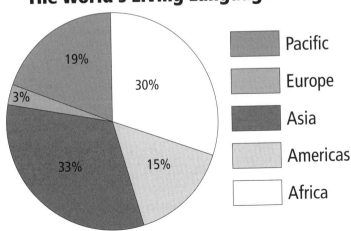

- Pacific
- Europe
- Asia
- Americas
- Africa

Appendices

Can a Language Recover?

The Linguistics Society of America (LSA) gives 1 million as the minimum number of speakers a language needs to be deemed secure from erosion, attrition, and eventual extinction. On the other hand, the LSA points out that for some languages looking at the actual number of speakers does not tell the whole story. Small tribal groups may have populations of 200 or less, with 95% speaking the tribal language as their native tongue. In this situation, an assessment of the relative health of the language can be difficult.

When a language is lost it is usually the result of a societal change. Language erosion in a community is difficult to reverse. A few languages that have undergone severe declines may be gaining speakers, or at least stabilizing in their numbers, with Welsh, Irish Gaelic, and Navajo as recent examples. In all three of these cases, recovery of the language is directly linked to overcoming a history of social and political oppression. Because many parents have not grown up speaking these languages, efforts to pass these languages on to children have been centered on teaching through the schools. There is some disagreement about the extent to which these languages are attracting new speakers who use the languages on a regular basis in their daily lives.

Appendices

Welsh

Welsh seems to be attracting new speakers, although the population of Wales has also been increasing, and the language has not been keeping pace. Welsh is taught in schools and also received a boost from the 1993 Welsh Language Act, although some language activists criticize the Act as being largely symbolic. According to U.K. census figures, in 1911 there were nearly 1 million speakers of Welsh in Wales. The number of speakers has declined over the last century to about a half million speakers.

In the 1960s the Welsh Language Society was formed and began campaigning, through protests and other forms of civil disobedience, for the Welsh language. Due in part to pressure from this and other groups, in the 1970s bilingual signage began to be used in Wales, and in 1982 a Welsh television channel began broadcasting. In 1991 the U.K. census found 508,098 speakers of Welsh, or 18.7% of the population of Wales. The Welsh Office in 1992 surveyed the population and found 368,000 fluent speakers, with an additional 94,900 who spoke the language fairly well, and another 467,300 who reported they could speak some Welsh. Although the 1993 Welsh Language Act stopped short of giving Welsh official status in Wales, it did make provisions for the use of Welsh in public life, i.e. in the court system.

According to U.K. census figures in 2001 there were 575,640 speakers of Welsh, or 20.5% of the population, with 28% the population reported to understand Welsh. In the past Welsh was considered more of a rural language, but the most recent census found that the language had gained speakers in urban areas, while continuing to decline in use in rural areas.

Appendices

Irish

The beginning of the decline in use of Irish in Ireland can be traced back to events in the sixteenth and seventeenth centuries. However, there were still an estimated four million speakers in 1835, mostly among the rural poor. As these were the people hit hardest by the potato famines of the 1800s, many of them were among those who emigrated, resulting in a significant drop in Irish speakers in Ireland. Irish remained in use in some communities in the west of Ireland, but 1926 census figures estimated there were only 540,802 Irish speakers in the country. The 1937 Constitution established Irish as an official language, with English as a second official language in Ireland. Irish is taught as a subject in school, and there are a few immersion schools in Irish.

According to Lelia Murtaghy, a researcher at the Linguistics Institute of Ireland, despite the fact that children in Ireland spend 13-14 years studying Irish as a school subject, not enough research has been done on whether their Irish language skills are maintained after graduation, and what the role of Irish is as a language in children's lives, other than a school subject. The chart below shows clearly that the number of people who would like, at least, to be identified as Irish speakers has increased.

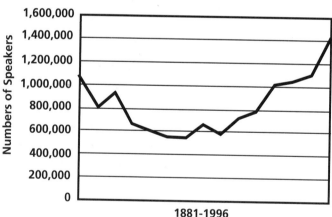

Change in Numbers of Speakers of Irish Gaelic in Ireland from 1861 to 1996

Data Source: Central Statistics Office Ireland

Appendices

Navajo

Whether or not Navajo, also known as Dine, will stabilize remains to be seen. According to the 1990 U.S. Census there were an estimated 148,530 speakers of Navajo in the United States, primarily in the Four Corners area of the Southwest, made up of parts of Arizona, New Mexico, Utah and Colorado. Out of a tribal population of about 220,000 the percentage of speakers of the tribal language is much higher than for most indigenous groups in the United States. Still, many fear the language is fading.

In their 1995 report for the Bilingual Research Journal, Agnes and Wayne Holm point out that despite the increase in interest in Navajo being taught in schools, the numbers of children who are entering school speaking Navajo as their first language has dropped dramatically since the early 1970s. Navajo has strong supporters, but the success to date of language education programs has been mixed. This is due in part to the lingering feeling among some Navajo that the language is of limited value, and that bringing up their children in Navajo could even hold them back. There is also no standardization of curriculum in the schools where it is taught because they are located in three different states, and a number of school districts.

Navajo had been used as a tool in a transitional program of education intended to teach children English upon school entry. However, by the mid- to late-1980s the majority of children entered school already speaking English, not Navajo, as their first language. Many did not speak any Navajo at all. Some schools began moving toward models of language education designed to teach Navajo as a heritage language to non-speakers. The language programs have taken different forms at different schools, but were generally described as bilingual education. Because of the special rights granted to reservations by federal law, bilingual education in Navajo and English has continued on reservations and in tribal schools, despite the passage of English-only measures in a number of southwestern states.

Appendices

According to Dr. Evangeline Yazzie-Parsons of Northern Arizona University and the Holms, many Navajo parents have either resigned themselves to the loss of their language, or view it as a low prestige language with limited utility for their children. On the other hand, when Arizona's Proposition 203, banning bilingual education, went to a vote, there was significant opposition to the measure in areas with large Native American populations. Another indication that the perceived value of Navajo among its own people may be increasing occurred when staff of an Arizona restaurant recently filed suit against the restaurant's owner, who had reportedly asked all employees to sign an agreement to speak English only at work.

Languages Spoken at Home in the United States

Most of the non-English languages spoken at home in the United States are not indigenous languages, but instead are languages that immigrants to this country bring with them. According to U.S. Census Bureau figures for the year 2000, the rate of immigration to the U.S. is at its highest rate since the 1850s. The number of U.S. residents who were born in another country was 32.5 million, by Census Bureau estimates for March of 2002.

32.5 million sounds like a large number of people, so it may seem surprising that, in the year 2000, only 17.9% of people aged 5 years or older living in the United States spoke a language other than English at home. In fact, the percentage of the population of the United States who immigrated is only 11.5%, less than the historic peak of 14.8% in 1890. On the other hand, in certain parts of the country, such as California and other parts of the Southwest, and in larger cities such as New York, the percentage of residents who were born outside the country is much higher.

Over half of U.S. residents born elsewhere, 51.7%, are from Latin America. Spanish is spoken at home by about 10% of the U.S. population. The number of people who emigrated from Asia has now surpassed the number from Europe with 26.4% of foreign-born residents coming from Asia, compared to 15.8% from Europe. Tagalog, the language of the Philippines, is now the sixth most commonly spoken language at home and the Chinese group of languages is gaining on the group made up of various varieties of French for third place.

Appendices

Languages Spoken at Home in the United States in 2000 by Residents Age 5 Years and Older

Language spoken at home	Number of speakers	Percentage of U.S. population
English only	215,423,557	82.1
Other languages	46,951,595	17.9
Spanish (incl. Spanish Creole)	28,101,052	10.7
French (includes Patois, Cajun, French Creole)	2,097,206	0.8
Chinese (all varieties)	2,022,143	0.8
German	1,383,442	0.5
Tagalog	1,224,241	0.5
Vietnamese	1,009,627	0.4
Italian	1,008,370	0.4
Korean	894,063	0.3
Russian	706,242	0.3
Polish	667,414	0.3
Arabic	614,582	0.2
Portuguese or Portuguese Creole	564,630	0.2
Japanese	477,997	0.2
Greek	365,436	0.1
Hindi	317,057	0.1

Data Source: U.S. Census Bureau

Dialects vs. Languages

In the previous table there are a number of speakers of dialect forms of various languages. What is the difference between a dialect and a language? Dialects are variations of a language, with pronunciation, grammar and vocabulary that differ in regular ways from the standard variety of the language. Speakers of different dialects of the same language are usually mutually intelligible. In other words, speakers of different dialects can understand one another, speakers of different languages can't. This seems fairly straightforward, but it's not. For one thing, there are forms of speech that could probably be defined as dialects that we call languages, and languages we call dialects.

Appendices

Generally speaking, decisions about where one language stops and another begins reflect political boundaries and the feeling of the people who live within them that they share a common culture and social history. For example, speakers of Mandarin, Wu, Cantonese, and other forms of Chinese use the same writing system, but different spoken languages, if defined in purely linguistic terms. Monolingual speakers of one variety of Chinese don't understand another. However, Mandarin, Wu, Cantonese, and the other varieties are referred to as dialects of Chinese for political and social reasons, and because they now share a writing system.

On the other hand, Swedish and Danish speakers can understand each with relative ease, so they could be said to be speaking dialects of the same language. The southern part of Sweden was claimed by Denmark until 1660, and it was said at that time that people there were speaking a dialect of Danish, rather than Swedish. These days we say that those living in the south of Sweden and those living in Denmark speak separate, although closely related languages.

Linguists may look to chains of intelligibility in trying to sort out languages and dialects. This is something like a game of Telephone, where the farther one gets from the starting point, the more the message changes. A person may understand someone living in a region just to the south of him, who might also understand the people living to the south of her, who would be completely incomprehensible to the first person. The idea is that there can be a continuum of a language that is represented by the chain of dialects. It is still complicated to use the chain of intelligibility to try to determine which dialects are part of what language because at one end of the chain, the dialect may resemble one recognized language, while at the other end it may more closely resemble another.

Sometimes people refer to dialect when they mean accent. In English, and many other languages, variation in how people pronounce vowel sounds varies by region. However, to distinguish dialect, linguists look for variations in grammar, too. Differences in vocabulary are less conclusive. In the United States, people who speak Standard American English may sit on couches, sofas, or even davenports, depending on their age, where they grew up, and where they live.

Appendices

People also have their own personal ideolects, or ways of speaking, that are a product of their personal language experiences and preferences. Many languages have some differences in the way that people of different genders speak. In bilingual families using the one person—one language approach, if gender differences in language use are significant and the gender of the parent speaking the language is different from that of the child, parents will need to make a decision about the importance of teaching the child these gender differences. In some cases, this can be hard to teach explicitly, but if there is enough exposure to different speakers of the language children will probably observe it themselves.

Appendix F

Resources for Less Commonly Spoken Languages

In terms of a family's ability to provide a language environment with contact with other speakers of the language, the opportunity to attend cultural events, access to media in the language, etc., it is obviously easier when there are a significant number of speakers nearby. For families whose minority language does not fall into the top twenty most widely spoken languages in the world, or even the top fifty, finding language resources can be a challenge. Here are some good places to start.

European Bureau for Lesser Used Languages
Rue Saint-Josse, 49 B-1210 Bruxelles
Tel: +32 2 218.25.90 Fax: +32 2 218.19.74
www.eblul.org
See description in Appendix A.

Appendices

Less Commonly Taught Languages Project
Center for Advanced Research on Language Acquisition (CARLA)
University of Minnesota
619 Heller Hall
Minneapolis, MN 55455-0110 USA
(612) 626-8600
www.carla.acad.umn.edu
Database on where to study less commonly taught languages, and information on materials.

Native Web
www.nativeweb.com
Web portal on indigenous culture around the world. Find "Languages and Linguistics" on the main page; click for a list of links on a variety of indigenous languages.

Sabhal Mor Ostaig
An Teanga, An t-Eilean Sgitheanach, Alba
IV44 8RQ UK
www.smo.uhi.ac.uk
The website of this Gaelic college located on the Isle of Skye in Scotland has an extensive list of links for minority languages in Europe.

UCLA Language Materials Project
University of California, Los Angeles
www.lmp.ucla.edu
See description in Appendix A, page 208.

Index